The IRISH WEDDING BOOK

For

_____

and

_____

who were engaged on

Date _____

Wedding Day

Date _____

Place _____

This book is lovingly dedicated
to Vivian, my husband,
who believed in and encouraged me
every step of the way.

The IRISH WEDDING BOOK

KIM McGUIRE

WOLFHOUND PRESS

First published 1994 by
Wolfhound Press
68 Mountjoy Square
Dublin 1

British Library Cataloguing in Publication Data

McGuire, Kim
    Irish Wedding Book: Everything You Need
    to Plan Your Wedding
    I. Title
    395

    ISBN 0-86327-376-9

Cover design: Joe Gervin
Cover photograph: Michael Kenny
Typesetting: Wolfhound Press
Printed in the Republic of Ireland by Colour Books

CONTENTS

Introduction

Congratulations! Getting married is a very happy occasion, and probably the single most important day in your lives. Of course, there will be other special events, but none quite like the moment the two of you stand in front of your families and friends exchanging your vows. But a wonderful wedding does not happen by chance — it requires forethought, patience and, above all, planning.

This book is designed to help you make the most of this exciting time together. It charts everything, from the moment you first announce your engagement to the day you return from honeymoon. In between times, it takes you through every stage — buying the rings, choosing your wedding attendants, picking a venue, meeting the celebrant, finding a florist — and the festivities that mark each stage, right up to the wedding and reception.

You will also find useful planning pages at the end of each chapter to keep all your wedding details in one place. No more searching through endless pieces of paper. Keeping your notes organised like this will give you more time to do things that really matter.

But probably the best reason for reading this book is to learn how to make your wedding just that little bit more special. No more boring celebrations. Each chapter is chock-full of creative ideas. For the groom there are ideas on dress hire, gifts for attendants and wedding rings. A chapter on do-it-yourself receptions offers recipes and great decorating tips. You will find that you can give a personal touch to just about anything — invitations, parties, cakes, music, transport and even flowers. The possibilities are endless.

So, enjoy this very special time together. Let this book do its job and take the worry out of planning your wedding. And most of all, have a great day.

> *All the best!*
> *Kim McGuire*

Acknowledgements

A book as complete as this is never done alone. In the past two years, many people and organisations have freely and patiently assisted me in my research, thus making this the best, most authoritative Irish wedding book. It is with much appreciation that I thank the following people and companies.

For their assistance in research material: Seamus MacMathúna of Comhaltas Ceoltoirí Eireann, Mrs Bee Mannix-Walsh of the Cookery Centre of Ireland; Robert C. Quinn of Weir & Sons; John Appleby of Appleby Jewellers, Keith Cusack of Jewel Casket; the Catholic Marriage Advisory Council; *The Irish Times; The Independent; The Cork Examiner; The Bray People,* Lantz Stationery, Louisa Maxwell for her expertise in wedding music, Liza's Florist, Celia Cave who let me in on a few floral secrets, and Martin Brown for his help in finding traditional Irish wedding music.

I am indebted to Fr Jim Corkery SJ for reviewing and correcting the section on Catholic weddings and to Fr William Fortune CC of Dalkey; Philip Jacob and Valerie O'Brien of the Religious Society of Friends for their assistance regarding the Quaker service and marriage customs; Steven H. Jensen, President Ireland Dublin Mission and Sister Janet Carrigan of the Church of Jesus Christ of Latter Day Saints for material on Mormon weddings; Chief Rabbi Harris and his assistant Hilda Solomons for the many telephone calls and guidance concerning Jewish celebrations; The Reverend Paul Colton, Rector, Castleknock & Mulhuddart with Clonsilla, for suggesting resources and editing the section on the Church of Ireland. To Olive Dawson for kindly taking my telephone calls and her expertise in registry weddings. I also wish to thank solicitor Pat Morrisey of L.K. Shields & Partners for his help concerning legal matters.

My friends, Tina Quinn, Niamh Morris, Elaine Comerford, Jackie Allen and Marguerite Sharpe also made the book possible by reading the manuscript and making changes, corrections and comments for its improvement.

Seamus Cashman, Josephine O'Donovan and everyone at Wolfhound Press worked to make this dream a reality. I am most thankful. And to Frances Power who edited the entire manuscript with care.

And last, but not least, a very special thanks to my dad, Douglas Manifold, for teaching me that nothing is impossible.

1 COUNTDOWN

Getting married is a lot of fun. In the months before the wedding and especially on the day, it is a time for joy, laughter and great happiness. But for couples who leave things to the last minute, a wedding is more like a meeting of two rivers — confusion, agitation and a flurry of excitement arise as the two come together. Couples are often amazed to learn that many churches, registry offices and reception venues must be booked six to twelve months in advance, that planning a ceremony takes more than one or two meetings with the celebrant and that caterers, florists, musicians and the like must be carefully advised. Avoiding such hassles is easy — all you have to do is get started early on.

For most people, your wedding is the largest and most complicated event you will ever have organised. It can also be the most fun! Whether you decide to gather all your friends and distant relatives or celebrate with a chosen few, this exciting change in your life happens on just one day — one that you will remember forever.

As the day draws nearer, you will be glad of the time you put into early plans. It is invaluable to have thought through the thorny questions of budgets, style of wedding, who to invite and so on, long before time and tempers get short. If at all possible, the two of you should decide privately exactly what you would like. Then, when parents, in laws and others make suggestions, you will each know what your partner thinks. This chapter outlines your starting points and helps you begin your planning.

As a general rule, you should begin by meeting your clergy or contacting the registry office to set a date. At your first meeting, pick three or four suitable days and times before committing yourself to anything definite. This will give you greater flexibility when booking a reception venue and will save dozens of phone calls back and forth.

Next contact various reception venues and check on availability. You will be expected to have a rough idea of the number of guests invited and it is always better to err on the high side. When you finish your invitation list you can always phone with the final head count.

The following is a list of wedding activities. Choose what you will need to do and keep track of each item by ticking it off when completed. The six-month planning calendar in this chapter will help you to remember important dates and appointments.

AS SOON AS POSSIBLE

_ Announce your engagement.

_ Contact your local clergy or registry office to set a date.

_ Determine your budget.

_ Send for brochures and menus from hotels, other possible reception venues, caterers and marquee companies.

_ Decide on the style of your wedding — formal or informal — and whether you will hold the reception at home or elsewhere.

SIX TO TWELVE MONTHS

_ Book reception venue and/or caterers.

_ Choose bridesmaids, best man, ushers and other attendants.

_ Register for pre-marriage course, if necessary.

_ Shop for wedding gown, bridesmaid and flower girl's dresses.

_ Choose wedding head-dress, accessories, jewellery, shoes.

_ Choose a colour scheme for the wedding.

_ Ask for time off from work for wedding and honeymoon.

_ Book honeymoon.

THREE TO SIX MONTHS

_ Compile guest list with both families and decide how many guests to invite to the ceremony, reception and afters.

_ Register at department store for wedding gifts.

_ Begin health and beauty regime.

_ Book contract services such as:
    musicians;
    florists;
    stationery;
    videographer and photographer.

_ Decide on clothes for groom, best man, ushers and ring bearer, arrange to hire them if necessary.

_ Choose your wedding rings.
_ Mothers and fathers should choose their wedding clothes.
_ Apply for passports.
_ Order the wedding cake if the hotel is not providing one.
_ Order Papal Blessing, if desired.
_ Consider taking out wedding insurance.

TWO MONTHS
_ Post the wedding invitations.
_ Confirm dates with contract services.
_ Co-ordinate menu and drinks plan for reception with hotel or caterer.
_ Firm up details with clergy or registry office.
_ Buy gifts for bridesmaids, best man, ushers and other attendants.
_ Arrange accommodation for out-of-town guests.
_ Shop for accessories.
_ See your doctor for a check-up.
_ Keep record of who accepts and declines invitations.

ONE MONTH
_ Contact hotel or caterer with final number of guests.
_ Choose going away outfit.
_ Plan seating arrangements for reception.
_ Make hair and make-up appointments.
_ Schedule final fittings for wedding gown and bridesmaid dresses.
_ Pick up honeymoon tickets.
_ Give photographer list of photographs to be taken.
_ Contact everyone in wedding party about rehearsal.
_ Organise going-away and honeymoon clothes.
_ Keep record of gifts received (for thank-you notes later).

ONE WEEK
_ Review final guest list and give numbers to caterer or hotel.
_ Pack for honeymoon.
_ Confirm all bookings.
_ Try on wedding gown with accessories.
_ Have full rehearsal: don't forget to time the journey from home to the ceremony.

THE DAY BEFORE

_ Schedule any beauty or grooming treatments.

_ Check luggage for honeymoon.

_ Arrange for honeymoon suitcases to be taken to the reception.

_ Give gifts to wedding attendants.

_ Pick up flowers for the ceremony and deliver.

_ Collect groom's suit and be sure other attendants have theirs.

_ Relax, you're almost there!

THE DAY

_ Give wedding rings to best man.

_ Have hair and make-up done.

_ Have fun.

AFTER THE WEDDING

_ Send cake to guests who could not attend.

_ Order wedding photos and video.

_ Pay any outstanding wedding bills.

_ Change all relevant documents to reflect change in name, if any, and marital status — bank account, credit cards, passport, driving licence, tax records, etc.

_ Review current insurance policies and change as necessary.

_ Contact a solicitor to write up a will.

_ Write thank-you notes.

_ Let the relevant people know of your change of address if any.

In folk tradition, the most popular time for marriage was Shrovetide.

SIX-MONTH PLANNER

Use these pages as a rough schedule for your wedding. Fill in the dates, beginning six months before the big day.

MONTH

Sunday	Sunday	Sunday
Monday	Monday	Monday
Tuesday	Tuesday	Tuesday
Wednesday	Wednesday	Wednesday
Thursday	Thursday	Thursday
Friday	Friday	Friday
Saturday	Saturday	Saturday

MONTH

Sunday	Sunday	Sunday	Sunday
Monday	Monday	Monday	Monday
Tuesday	Tuesday	Tuesday	Tuesday
Wednesday	Wednesday	Wednesday	Wednesday
Thursday	Thursday	Thursday	Thursday
Friday	Friday	Friday	Friday
Saturday	Saturday	Saturday	Saturday

MONTH			
Sunday	Sunday	Sunday	Sunday
Monday	Monday	Monday	Monday
Tuesday	Tuesday	Tuesday	Tuesday
Wednesday	Wednesday	Wednesday	Wednesday
Thursday	Thursday	Thursday	Thursday
Friday	Friday	Friday	Friday
Saturday	Saturday	Saturday	Saturday

MONTH			
Sunday	Sunday	Sunday	Sunday
Monday	Monday	Monday	Monday
Tuesday	Tuesday	Tuesday	Tuesday
Wednesday	Wednesday	Wednesday	Wednesday
Thursday	Thursday	Thursday	Thursday
Friday	Friday	Friday	Friday
Saturday	Saturday	Saturday	Saturday

MONTH

Sunday	Sunday	Sunday
Monday	Monday	Monday
Tuesday	Tuesday	Tuesday
Wednesday	Wednesday	Wednesday
Thursday	Thursday	Thursday
Friday	Friday	Friday
Saturday	Saturday	Saturday

MONTH

Sunday	Sunday	Sunday	Sunday
Monday	Monday	Monday	Monday
Tuesday	Tuesday	Tuesday	Tuesday
Wednesday	Wednesday	Wednesday	Wednesday
Thursday	Thursday	Thursday	Thursday
Friday	Friday	Friday	Friday
Saturday	Saturday	Saturday	Saturday

2   YOUR ENGAGEMENT

In the days of matchmaking, when Irish weddings were often arranged like business deals, little thought was given to the actual engagement. In fact, it was not unheard of for the couple to meet for the first time only a week before their marriage.

Two or three nights before the wedding day, the groom would arrive at the bride's house for a celebration. Friends and neighbours of the bride's family would be invited and dancing, drinking and singing would last well into the night and into the next day.

Although this kind of celebration exists elsewhere today, getting engaged in Ireland is now a much more intimate moment for a couple. Sometimes, the decision is a mutual one that just seems to evolve naturally. Other times, the man plans the engagement as a surprise and buys a ring in secrecy, waiting for the right moment to propose. In the next chapter, you will find more information on selecting and buying the engagement ring. And every so often, it is the woman who pops the question. Still, even in these relatively informal times, good manners require that certain formalities are followed in spreading the good news.

ANNOUNCING THE ENGAGEMENT

The first people to be told should be both sets of parents. There is no longer any need for the groom-to-be to request a meeting with the bride's father to humbly ask for her hand in marriage. Nowadays, the couple usually tell their parents that they have decided to get married and ask for their 'blessing'. This is best done together and in person. You might like to mark the occasion by bringing along champagne or sparkling wine so that everyone can toast your future.

If your parents live far away, a telephone call or letter from both of you should be made or sent as soon as possible. Think how hurt your parents would be to learn of your engagement from someone else. And, if you can, try to organise a get-together before your wedding to introduce your family to your partner.

Once both your families have been told, they should get to know one another. According to tradition, the groom's parents invite the bride's family to dinner at their house or at a restaurant. If the bride's parents are separated or no longer living, the groom's parents should extend the invitation to the person who raised her, or another close living relative. Similarly, if the groom's parents are separated, his mother should issue the invitation and include, when possible, his father. If the groom's mother is no longer living, his father or sister can make the overture.

When a meeting is out of the question due to distance or other commitments, the groom's mother should write a letter, on behalf of her family, to the bride's family expressing their delight over your announcement. Sometimes, for various reasons, the groom's family may not make the first contact. Don't let this formality stand in the way. It is perfectly acceptable for the bride's family to contact the groom's, or for the two of you to extend an invitation to both sets of parents. Don't stand on ceremony — this is a time for celebration!

Are your parents already friendly? Then this is a perfect excuse for them to get together again. Or perhaps they are acquainted but not close friends. If you feel there may be friction between your families, iron out the differences now before complicated wedding arrangements begin. If there is a problem, each of you should speak separately to your parents. Explain how important it is to you that there are good relations between the families and ask them to help in the smooth running of the events leading up to the wedding day.

Good friends and close relatives should be the next to know about your engagement. It is best to contact everyone at roughly the same time to avoid hurting anyone's feelings. If someone special lives far away, a telephone call or a note is a thoughtful way of showing how important they are to you. This should be timed to coincide with any public announcements — even those living far away should not learn of your plans by word-of-mouth or read them in the newspaper.

GETTING TO KNOW YOUR IN-LAWS

Some people prefer to keep their future in-laws at a distance for fear that they may get too involved in the wedding plans! Jokes about meddlesome mothers-in-law abound. In reality, parents rarely cause problems and when they do it is usually because they are desperately interested in their children's lives. The best way to ensure a good relationship with your new in-laws is to spend a little time getting to know them.

If you have your own flat or home, the easiest way to break the ice is to invite your future in-laws over for an informal meal. Nothing fancy is the secret to success. If you can't have people over, organise a night out at a restaurant or pub where you can talk without being interrupted or having to shout over loud music. Otherwise choose an outing that gives you all a chance to chat together.

Deciding what to call your in-laws can be a delicate subject. If they haven't already broached the subject, the best approach is to pluck up your courage and be direct. Something like, 'Mr/Mrs Morris, now that John/Ann and I are getting married, I was wondering if I might call you Dad/Mum or Dan/Elaine?' This will certainly break the ice and give them a chance to voice their preference.

THE NEWSPAPER ANNOUNCEMENT

Announcing your engagement in the *Irish Times*, the *Irish Independent*, or a local newspaper is popular these days. For a couple who live away from home, outside Ireland, or who have a large circle of business colleagues, an announcement is well worth the expense. The cost ranges from £10 to £100, depending on the paper.

To place an announcement, contact the advertising department of the paper. Enquire about their rates, deadline for placing the notice, which day of the week the announcement will run, whether there is a standard format the paper follows and, if so, what information is required. Some papers will print a photograph of you both, in which case ask whether they require black and white or colour, glossy or matt, and the size. If you are sending a photograph you want returned, write your name and address on a sticky label and put it on the reverse side. Some newspapers will not return your photo, others will ask you to include a self-addressed stamped envelope. Check the paper's policy before you part with your favourite shot.

Paying for the announcement is traditionally the responsibility of the bride's family but very often the bride or the couple themselves see to the expense. If yours is to be a formal wedding, and the bride's parents are overseeing the expenses, the announcement should reflect this decision and read as follows:

MR M. F. BROPHY

MISS S.N. MURPHY

Mr and Mrs Vincent Murphy

of 11 Green Street, Blackrock, County Dublin

are pleased to announce the

engagement of their daughter

Sinead Noreen

to

Martin Francis

second son of Mr and Mrs Richard Brophy

of 134 Mount Street, Bray, County Wicklow

If Martin is the eldest, third, fourth, son of Mr and Mrs Richard Brophy, alter the notice to suit.

If you prefer something more informal, or both of you are paying for the wedding, your announcement might read:

MARTIN BROPHY

SINEAD MURPHY

Martin and Sinead

together with their families

are delighted to announce their engagement

or

Mr Martin Brophy

Miss Sinead Murphy

The engagement is announced between Martin,

son of Mr and Mrs Richard Brophy

134 Mount Street, Bray, County Wicklow

and

Sinead

daughter of Mr and Mrs Vincent Murphy

11 Green Street, Blackrock, County Dublin

If either or both of you is an officer in the Army or Gardaí, your rank, branch of service and any other relevant information may be included, for example:

Commander Martin Brophy

Miss Sinead Murphy

The engagement is announced between Sinead

only daughter of Mr and Mrs Vincent Murphy

11 Green Street, Blackrock, County Dublin

and

Martin,

second son of Mr and Mrs Richard Brophy

134 Mount Street, Bray, County Wicklow

If the bride is a widow or the groom a widower, it is a nice idea to mention this:

Mr Martin Brophy

Ms Sinead Murphy Byrne

The engagement is announced between Martin,

second son of Mr and Mrs Richard Brophy

134 Mount Street, Bray, County Wicklow

and

Sinead

daughter of Mr and Mrs Vincent Murphy

11 Green Street, Blackrock, County Wicklow

and widow of the late Mr John Byrne

If either of your parents are divorced, remarried, or if one of them has died, you may wish to make this clear:

Mr Martin Brophy

Miss Sinead Murphy

The engagement is announced between Sinead

daughter of Mr Vincent Murphy of Blackrock, County Dublin

and the late Mrs Ann Murphy

and

Martin,

son of Mr Richard Brophy of Bray, County Wicklow

and Mrs Maureen O'Reilly of Terenure, County Dublin

When placing press announcements, do be careful of a growing problem — burglars. By placing your announcement in a newspaper, you may be inadvertently inviting some unwanted guests interested only in the gifts you will receive. To avoid this potential problem, try using this format:

MR. M.F. BROPHY
MISS S.N. MURPHY
Mr and Mrs Vincent Murphy
of Blackrock, County Dublin
are pleased to announce the
engagement of their daughter
Sinead Noreen
to
Martin Francis
son of Mr and Mrs Richard Brophy
of Bray, County Wicklow

Alternatively, you could always ask someone you trust to stay at the house on your wedding day to watch over your gifts, or, better still, move them to a different address.

Use the following space to write out your announcement:

THE ENGAGEMENT PARTY

After telling your family and friends about your engagement, they may want to get together to congratulate you and celebrate your plans. An engagement party, which can be hosted by either of your families, close friends, or even yourselves, is an ideal way for everyone to get to know your partner and to share in your festive mood. And the best thing about an engagement party is there are no rules: you are free to plan as you wish. You can be ultra formal and send out engraved invitations or telephone a few good friends and have them over, or meet in the local pub. Theme parties are a great idea. For example, if you like the outdoors or country western music, then a barbecue is perfect. Send invitations that read: 'Martin and Sinead are getting hitched!', play your favourite music, serve baked beans, potato salad, barbecued steaks, chicken and cold beer.

When speeches are made during an engagement party, there are a few rules of etiquette to follow. Traditionally, if the bride's parents are paying for the wedding, the father of the bride starts by toasting his daughter and his future son-in-law. He may, if he chooses, mention a few moments in her childhood which he remembers fondly. If the bride's father is deceased, her mother, brother, sister, favourite uncle or family friend can make the speech instead. The groom-to-be then replies with a toast thanking his fiancée's family and toasting the health of everyone present. After this, the groom's father is welcome to make a speech, as are friends and guests of the couple.

ENGAGEMENT PRESENTS

Engagement presents should never be expected, but the chances are that you will probably receive several small gifts from family and close friends. Usually, these are token presents which are fun or which can be used by the two of you in your new home. Be sure to send handwritten notes to thank people as quickly as possible. Ideally, you should do this immediately after opening a present, while your excitement is still fresh. Since this isn't always possible, try not to let more than a week pass without seeing to it.

GETTING ORGANISED EARLY

This first party is a good time to start organising yourself. Buy some 3 x 5" index cards and designate one card for each person you invite to the party. On the card put the person's name, address, telephone number and other useful information. Later, as your guests begin to reply, you can note on the card whether they accept your invitation. If someone gives you a gift be sure to write down what it was and when you sent a thank-you note.

    Example

    Mr and Mrs William O'Brien (Bill and Noelle)

    154 South County Road

    Blackrock, County Dublin Telephone: 634-4567

    Engagement Party: Accepts

    Gift: Vase

    Thank-you sent: 11/3/96

This may seem a bit over-the-top at this stage but, as you become more involved in preparations, you will be surprised at how easy it is to forget who sent what and whether you thanked them properly. Writing everything down in one place will make life much less complicated in an already busy time.

If you are planning your own engagement party, use the planner at the end of this chapter to sort out the details and to record the guest list. After the party, use the gift organiser in chapter 13 to keep track of the gifts you receive.

BROKEN ENGAGEMENT

A broken engagement is very painful for everyone involved, but it is much better to end a troubled relationship before a wedding rather than after. If the engagement was announced in the newspaper, the bride's family should place a brief notice in the same paper, as follows:

    The marriage arranged between

    John Murphy and Ann O'Brien

    will not now take place.

or

Mr and Mrs Sean O'Brien
announce that the marriage of their daughter
Ann Margaret
to
Mr John Francis Murphy
will not now take place.

Close friends and relatives should be contacted by letter or telephone and all wedding presents should be returned. No details need be given. In return, friends and family should send a kind note, acknowledging the broken engagement.

If the bride breaks off the engagement, she should return, or at least offer to return, the ring to the groom. If, however, the groom cancels the wedding, the bride has the right, by custom, to keep the ring and may continue to wear it on her other hand.

If wedding invitations have gone out, they should be cancelled immediately by the bride's family. If time allows, a printed card in the same style as the invitation should be sent to all guests, accompanied by any gifts received. The wording should read as for the newspaper announcement. In other words, if you have chosen a formal style then the cancellation notes should be formal too. When there is not enough time to send cards, guests should be contacted by telephone or a handwritten note.

POSTPONEMENT OR CANCELLATION

Should the wedding be cancelled or postponed due to an illness or death in the family, an announcement should be made as follows:

Mr and Mrs Sean O'Brien announce that
owing to the illness of Mrs David Murphy
they are obliged to postpone
the marriage of their daughter
Ann Margaret
to
Mr John Francis Murphy
which was to have taken place
Saturday, 11th July 1996, to Saturday, 28th August 1996
The time and place remain the same.

or

Mr and Mrs Sean O'Brien
regret that they are obliged to recall*
the invitation to the marriage of their daughter
Ann Margaret
to
Mr John Francis Murphy
owing to the death of Mr Murphy's father
Mr David Murphy

* Cancel can be substituted for recall, if preferred.

The following lines can be added at the end:
The ceremony will be held privately
in the presence of the immediate family.

At the seventh-century Kilmaolcheadar church near Dingle stands an ogham pillar with a circular opening near the top. Legend has it that a couple are engaged if they join fingers through this hole.

ENGAGEMENT PARTY PLANNER

If you are organising your own engagement party, use this page to keep track of the details:

Host/Hostess _____

Date _____ Time _____ Theme _____

Location _____ Number of guests _____

Food _____

_____

_____

Company _____

Contact _____ Tel. _____

Drinks _____

_____

_____

Company _____

Contact _____ Tel. _____

Decorations _____

_____

_____

GUEST LIST

_____

_____

_____

_____

_____

_____

NOTES

3   ENGAGEMENT & WEDDING RINGS

The giving of rings has been a part of the marriage ceremony for centuries. The first recorded marriage rings date back to the days when early man tied plaited grass circlets around the bride's wrists and ankles to keep her spirit from running away. In ancient Egypt, grooms paid the bride's parents for the honour of marrying their daughter, and gold rings were given in part payment. Gold was chosen because of its great value and the ease with which it could be evaluated. But it wasn't until the medieval period that the engagement ring first appeared and came to symbolise the groom's honourable intentions and his right to court his betrothed in public.

Much has changed since those days, but it is still the bride who wears the engagement ring. Traditionally, and as portrayed in Hollywood golden oldies, the man buys a ring and proposes. But these days, most women prefer to participate in choosing an engagement ring. It is after all the one piece of jewellery a woman will wear almost every day for the rest of her life. Some couples do without an engagement ring altogether, preferring to spend the money on something else. This, of course, is perfectly acceptable so long as the bride doesn't mind! Any decision to dispense with a ring must come from her. No matter what you decide to do, remember there is no right or wrong. Whether you buy a ring or not is a personal decision — that is what makes marriage so unique. Each of us goes about it differently.

THE ENGAGEMENT RING

The most popular type of engagement ring in Ireland today is a solitaire (single) diamond, in a medium height, 18-carat yellow gold setting. Next, is the three-stone diamond setting. While diamond engagement rings are beautiful their costs, especially for high quality stones, can be a real drawback. Other stones worth considering are birthstones or semi-precious gems. Rubies, emeralds and pearls can be as expensive as diamonds but sapphires, opals and amethysts are usually less expensive but equally stunning. The following table gives the month, stone and its special meaning:

BIRTHSTONES

Month	Stone	Meaning
January	Garnet	Truth
February	Amethyst	Sincerity
March	Bloodstone/Aquamarine	Courage
April	Diamond	Purity
May	Emerald	Success
June	Pearl	Health
July	Ruby	Passion
August	Sardonyx	Happiness
September	Sapphire	Wisdom
October	Opal	Hope
November	Topaz	Fidelity
December	Turquoise/Lapis	Harmony

Brides preferring something out of the ordinary might like an antique ring. Many are more ornate and decorative than modern designs. The very popular Edwardian ring is perfect for active women because the stones sit flat within the setting, making it less likely to catch on clothing or scratch surfaces. The late Victorian style is known for its high and sometimes round settings and is a beautiful ring for women with large hands.

Another option is to have a ring designed specially for you. Sketch out a few rough ideas on paper or cut some pictures you like out of a magazine and take them to a reputable jeweller. You will find most are easy to work with and don't mind if you supply your own gems. Because your ring will probably be hand-detailed you should be prepared to pay more. Talk to a few jewellers about the costs involved so that you can compare prices.

You might also be offered a ring by your parents or another close relative. Of course, you should accept the ring if it's something you truly love. If not, try to turn down the offer tactfully, perhaps saying that you've always wanted a ring selected specially for you.

DIAMONDS

The first diamond engagement ring was presented to Mary of Burgundy in 1477 by her beloved Archduke Maximilian of Austria. Since then, the diamond, often referred to as brilliant, durable, everlasting — in fact, all the things one hopes love will be — has become the most popular engagement ring in the world.

If you are buying a diamond, especially if it is to be an investment, you need to know a little bit about them. There are four characteristics that determine the quality of a stone.

Colour: Or rather the whiteness of the stone — not the light reflected from it. Although most diamonds have some colour, the higher the quality of the stone, the less evident the colour. Ask a jeweller to review the International Colour Grading System with you before you purchase a diamond.

Cut: Often confused with the 'setting' of a diamond. The cut actually refers to the number of facets cut into the stone — usually fifty-eight — which reflect light throughout the stone, giving it more sparkle.

Clarity: All diamonds contain flaws (also known as inclusions), but the fewer the flaws the better. Flaws interfere with light passing through the stone and so make it appear less brilliant.

Carat: The size and weight of a diamond are measured in carats, each carat is made up of a hundred points. Therefore, a one-and-a-half carat diamond is made up of a hundred and fifty points. The size of a diamond is the most obvious factor in determining its value, but big is not necessarily better. Keep in mind that it is best to buy a small diamond of good quality rather than a large one of lesser quality.

RING SETTINGS

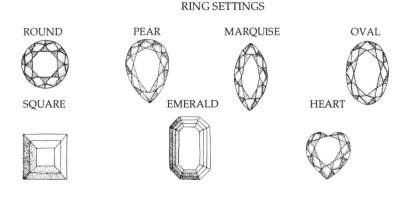

ROUND   PEAR   MARQUISE   OVAL

SQUARE   EMERALD   HEART

GOLD

Gold is measured in units called carats, on a scale of twenty-four. The higher the unit, the purer and softer the gold. For example, in Ireland most jewellery comes in 9c, 18c, and 24c (the use of 14c has recently been introduced). Diamonds, because of their value, are usually set in 18c — a quality gold that is not too soft. For men's rings, 9c gold is used because its hardness makes it capable of withstanding tough treatment and scratching without showing the wear and tear of a less sturdy, purer gold.

Gold also comes in several colours — red (often called rose), white, or yellow. The variations in colour are a result of alloys being introduced into the gold while it is in its molten form. Because of the extra work involved you can expect to pay more for a rose or white gold. However, you may not be getting value for money, while rose and white are unusual and lovely, yellow gold actually maintains its brilliance and shine much longer.

Platinum is another precious metal which can be used in ring making. Although similar in colour to white gold, it is a superior metal because it is harder, heavier, and less likely to show signs of wear over time. Platinum was very popular once, but is so expensive these days that jewellers rarely use it. You pay more for platinum's benefits but if you are buying a ring as an investment it is worth considering.

HOW TO BUY YOUR RINGS

Traditionally, the man buys the engagement ring for his fiancée and later the couple select wedding bands together. This way of getting engaged is particularly endearing to true romantics but may unnerve more practically minded women, who prefer to participate in selecting their engagement ring. For this reason it is advisable for a man to pre-arrange an exchange policy with a jeweller to return the ring for another or to present his intended with a substitute ring while proposing. Later, they can go in together to select the engagement ring and wedding bands.

Before you visit a jeweller, try to estimate how much you want to spend. This makes things much easier and more relaxing not just for both of you but for the sales person as well.

Next, consider your lifestyle. If you are an active person or work with your hands, a ring that is big and bulky may not be for you. Will you wear your rings all the time? If so, consider using 9c gold which is stronger and will withstand constant wear better than a purer gold, and it looks just as good.

With your price range and lifestyle in mind, start visiting a few jewellery shops together. The first few trips, try on several different styles to find one that suits your hand. Don't worry about not knowing your ring size; every jeweller will measure your finger regardless. If you have questions, feel free to ask them. A good jeweller won't mind investing time in you. When buying a woman's wedding ring, be sure that the gold content is compatible with that of the engagement ring. (Both rings should have the same carat value.) If one gold is harder than the other, the softer ring will, over time, become damaged by the constant rubbing and knocking of the two rings.

Be sure to ask for a receipt and insurance valuation document when you pay for your rings. Check that the receipt is written up in full with a proper description. Take a photograph or make a photocopy of the ring and attach it to the receipt for identification purposes. As soon as possible, insure them. Because jewellery is an item whose value changes, it is a good idea to get a new valuation every three to five years and submit it to your insurance company.

However you decide to choose your rings, make this a fun outing. Take time to have lunch or stop in a pub for a celebration drink. Whatever you do, don't rush your decision. For a bit of extra fun, take along a camera and snap some memories for your album.

THE WEDDING RING

Engagement rings seem to get all the glory but the real star on the day is the wedding ring. These days, wedding bands come in a multitude of styles for men and women.

Most men prefer a plain 9c gold band. It is simple, durable and can withstand fairly harsh treatment. You can choose from many colours, several widths and designs. If a traditional ring does not appeal to you, consider a claddagh, signet, or perhaps a tri-gold ring which is a traditional French wedding ring made of three different coloured gold bands which are twisted together.

Women, of course, have an even larger selection to choose from than men. There are gold bands, diamond eternity rings, multi-stone eternity rings, rings to fit neatly next to your engagement ring, and more.

If you are thinking about buying an antique ring, bear in mind that older wedding bands are considerably wider than today's fashionable width and are usually updated by being cut down or in half. If you find a ring that you both like, have it cut in half — one for each of you.

CARING FOR YOUR RINGS

The best way to care for your rings is to have them professionally cleaned or to clean them yourself with a commercial solution, available at most jewellery stores.

For a homemade remedy, steep your rings in an egg cup filled with whiskey or brandy, or mix one spoonful of liquid detergent in a cup of lukewarm water. Soak the ring for five minutes. Then with a small, soft toothbrush (or nail brush) carefully work the dirt loose from the stone. Homemade solutions should not be used on pearls, opals or emeralds as they are fragile and can easily shatter or lose their natural colour. Anyone with a diamond ring soon learns that they attract grease and dirt. Clean them regularly to keep them sparkling.

Gold jewellery can be brightened by scrubbing gently with toothpaste and a soft brush or toothbrush. After brushing, dip in a solution of liquid detergent and lukewarm water, follow with a rinse of lukewarm water and pat dry with a clean cloth. When you're cleaning your ring, check that the stones are all securely in place. Over time, the gold can become damaged, particularly on the claws and underside.

A bride and groom to be should never wash their hands in the same basin at the same time — it's courting disaster. (Irish tradition)

RING PLANNING

Bride's ring size   Groom's ring size

WEDDING RINGS

Favourite Selections

Shop	*Description*	*Price £*

Final Selection:

Style

Shop

Address

Contact   Tel.

Cost £   Deposit £   Balance Due

ENGAGEMENT RING

Favourite Selections

Shop	*Description*	*Price £*

Final Selection:

Style

Shop

Address

Contact   Tel.

Cost £   Deposit £   Balance Due

4   CAREFUL BUDGETING

You have shared the good news with your family and friends; now it's time to get down to the practical side of planning a wedding — the dreaded budget! Ideally, this should be done as early as possible. This needn't be a chore, so make it fun. Send out for pizza, open a bottle of Chianti and get to work! Decide which elements of the ceremony and reception are important to you both and which you don't mind doing away with. Once you know exactly what you want, you'll be ready to start costing.

TYPICAL BREAKDOWN OF EXPENSES

This covers three types of no-frill wedding, each with a hundred guests, one bridesmaid and one flower girl. The honeymoon is excluded as costs vary so dramatically.

	Simple	Moderate	Expensive
Announcement	£10	£100	£100
Bride's dress	£350	£575	£1,000
Headdress	£20	£35	£75
Shoes	£15	£50	£100
Hair/nails/make-up	£20	£50	£100
Groom's suit	£30	£50	£70
Engagement ring	£500	£1,500	£3,000
Two wedding rings	£150	£300	£500
Photos/video	£400	£750	£850
Music (ceremony and reception)	£150	£400	£800
Transport	£90	£100	£250
Bridesmaid's outfit	£150	£200	£250
Flower girl's outfit	£100	£150	£200
Stationery	£175	£250	£550

Cake	£100	£180	£250
Reception	£1,500	£5,000	£7,000
Flowers	£75	£150	£1,000
Going away outfit	£60	£150	£300
TOTAL	£3,895	£9,990	£16,395

As you can see, costs vary greatly according to the type of wedding, and expenses can quickly mount up. Use the planner at the end of this chapter to budget your wedding and keep track of costs.

Your budget will be influenced by the time of day the wedding takes place, the number of guests and the wedding's style or theme. For instance, do you want a big white wedding with two hundred guests and a sit-down dinner? Or, would you prefer to have a mid-day ceremony followed by an at-home buffet lunch for a hundred guests? You might decide smaller is better and invite only your immediate family and close friends to the ceremony and then to an intimate brunch.

Once you agree on the type of wedding you want, you should both talk to your parents. Let them know what you prefer and, if possible, discuss the costs involved. In the end the two of you will decide which ideas to use and which to do away with, but it is always good to make your parents feel included in the planning stages. No doubt, they will have some suggestions and ideas too. This is also a good time to discuss how the wedding will be paid for.

The tradition is that the bride's father pays most of the expenses. This custom dates from the days (not so long ago) when parents gave their sons an education and expected their daughters to marry well. Fortunately, times have changed. Nowadays, when parents pay for their daughter's wedding it is a sign of their love — not as part of a dowry.

WHO PAYS FOR WHAT?

The custom is that the bride's family pays for most of the expenses related to the wedding with the exception of the rings, the honeymoon and small items like flowers for the wedding party which are covered by the groom. As you can see from the breakdown of expenses, even the simplest of weddings can be expensive. For this reason the traditional rules on who pays for what are bending.

Some couples put off getting married until they are financially secure, so that they can pay for all or part of the celebration themselves. And, more and more often, the groom's family want to be involved in the planning of their son's wedding and will offer to contribute towards the cost.

Traditionally, though, wedding expenses are broken down as follows:

THE FATHER OF THE BRIDE
- Press announcements
- Invitations and other stationery
- Bride's wedding outfit and trousseau
- Bridesmaids' dresses
- Flowers for the ceremony and reception
- Transportation for bride and bridesmaids to the ceremony
- Music for the reception
- Reception
- Wedding cake
- Photographs and video

THE BRIDE
- Groom's wedding ring
- Groom's gift

THE GROOM
- Bride's engagement and wedding ring
- Transportation for himself, best man and groomsmen (if any) to the ceremony, and for bride and himself afterwards
- Flowers for bride, bridesmaids, flower girl, parents of the bride and groom and for himself, his groomsmen and ushers (if any)
- Music for the ceremony
- Church fees
- Presents for best man, groomsmen, ushers and ring bearer (if any)
- Gifts for bridesmaids and flower girls (if any)
- Present for bride
- Honeymoon

THE BRIDESMAIDS, GROOMSMEN AND USHERS
- Travel arrangements and accommodation, if living far away

SHARING THE COSTS

There are many ways to share wedding expenses. If the groom's parents want to help, this offer should be very tactfully made. It is then up to the bride's family to accept or decline as, regardless of the financial arrangements, the bride's parents are still the hosts of the wedding.

If the bride's parents agree, there are several ways to share the costs. Both sets of parents and the two of you might contribute a third of the costs each. Or, one set of parents could pay for the ceremony, while the two of you handle the honeymoon, and all of you share the reception expenses. Alternatively, the bride's parents could cover the majority of the costs and let the groom's parents pay for the flowers, beer, wine and spirits, transportation and music. Whatever agreement you come to, make sure that all parties feel comfortable with the arrangement as nothing sours an atmosphere more quickly than squabbles over bills.

WAYS TO CONTROL COSTS

Besides sharing the costs, there are many things you can do to actually reduce them. For instance, pare down your guest list. Don't include children under the age of seven, or invite only immediate family and close friends. If a sit-down dinner is too expensive, consider a brunch or tea reception. Serve savoury (paté, salmon, quiche) and sweet (tarts, trifle, fresh fruit) hors d'oeuvres, or hot entrées like crepes and quiche. Instead of hiring a big band or disco, opt for a piano player and possibly a vocalist. If any of your friends have special talents such as photography, baking, singing, dressmaking, etc., you might be able to press them into service. They might even offer their skills free as their wedding present to you.

If your mother's wedding dress fits, ask if you can wear it. Your mother will be proud to see you walking down the aisle in her gown. If you're planning a pre-wedding get-together with your grooms-men and bridesmaids, have it at home. It's cosier that way and everyone will get to know one another more quickly. Let your church flowers do double duty and use them at the reception. Just make sure to assign a trusted friend to move them after photographs have been taken.

MONEY-SAVING IDEAS

Be flexible and creative! Here are thirty-five ways to keep costs down.

1. Have your bridesmaid party at home
2. Have your dress made by a talented friend
3. Hire your wedding gown and veil
4. Hire bridesmaid and flower girl dresses
5. Hire mother's dress
6. Rent your dinner jacket
7. Buy pre-printed invitations
8. Type your own Order of Service or Mass booklet
9. Handwrite your invitations instead of using calligraphy
10. Invite only relatives and friends who remain close to both of you
11. Don't invite children under the age of seven
12. Don't encourage single friends to bring casual guests
13. Don't invite any business-related guests
14. Don't put your engagement announcement in the paper
15. Do the flowers yourself
16. Ask about locally grown flowers
17. Consider using dried flowers
18. Be dramatic and carry a single lily
19. Tie white or coloured ribbons to the pews instead of flowers
20. Put flowers on every second pew or on the first five only
21. Let flowers do double duty at the ceremony and reception
22. Have a brunch or tea reception instead of dinner
23. Have the reception in someone's house or garden
24. Rent a hall for the reception instead of a hotel
25. Have a cake and drinks only reception
26. Serve punch for the drinks reception
27. Serve a sparkling wine for the toasts instead of champagne
28. As opposed to a free bar, have a cash bar at the reception
29. Make the cake yourself
30. Make the food for the reception yourself
31. Instead of a band, hire a piano player or use taped music or CDs
32. Ask for a discount or free bridal suite when you book a hotel
33. Book your honeymoon flight for midweek rather than weekend
34. Choose an off-season destination for your honeymoon
35. Know the cancellation and refund policy for all vendors

Obviously, as with any discussion of money, the opportunity for conflict may arise. If you keep your wits about you and are willing to compromise then your family will follow suit. Keep a sense of proportion — you are embarking on a relationship to last forever and this ceremony is a celebration of your love. The size and grandeur of the wedding are secondary to the ceremony that binds you.

BUDGET PLANNER

Use this guide by crossing off the items you don't need and filling out the ones you do need, putting approximate costs in the estimate row. As you find out what the actual costs are, compare the difference and see how close you were (use the *Golden Pages* to phone around for estimates).

Number of guests _____   Total budget £ _____

	Estimated Cost	Actual Cost
THE ENGAGEMENT		
Engagement ring	£ _____	£ _____
Engagement announcement	£ _____	£ _____
Engagement party	£ _____	£ _____
Catering, refreshments/drink	£ _____	£ _____
Decorations, music	£ _____	£ _____
Other	£ _____	£ _____
Total	£ _____	£ _____
STATIONERY		
Engagement invitations	£ _____	£ _____
Wedding invitations	£ _____	£ _____
Envelopes	£ _____	£ _____
Evening invitations	£ _____	£ _____
Order of Service books	£ _____	£ _____
Thank-you cards	£ _____	£ _____
Napkins	£ _____	£ _____
Napkin rings	£ _____	£ _____
Place cards	£ _____	£ _____
Cake boxes	£ _____	£ _____
Envelope seals	£ _____	£ _____
Matchboxes	£ _____	£ _____
Postage	£ _____	£ _____
Other	£ _____	£ _____
Total	£ _____	£ _____
BRIDE'S CLOTHES		
Wedding dress	£ _____	£ _____
Veil	£ _____	£ _____

	Estimated Cost	Actual Cost
Lingerie	£ _____	£ _____
Shoes	£ _____	£ _____
Gloves	£ _____	£ _____
Jewellery	£ _____	£ _____
Make-up	£ _____	£ _____
Beauty treatments	£ _____	£ _____
Trousseau	£ _____	£ _____
Other	£ _____	£ _____
Total	£ _____	£ _____

GROOM'S CLOTHES

Dinner jacket or suit	£ _____	£ _____
Shirt	£ _____	£ _____
Shoes	£ _____	£ _____
Accessories	£ _____	£ _____
Other	£ _____	£ _____
Total	£ _____	£ _____

CEREMONY

Officiant	£ _____	£ _____
Bride's ring	£ _____	£ _____
Groom's ring	£ _____	£ _____
Music	£ _____	£ _____
Flowers	£ _____	£ _____
Rice/rose petals	£ _____	£ _____
Other	£ _____	£ _____
Total	£ _____	£ _____

WEDDING RECEPTION

Venue	£ _____	£ _____
Food	£ _____	£ _____
Beverages	£ _____	£ _____
Cake	£ _____	£ _____
Decorations	£ _____	£ _____
Music	£ _____	£ _____
Flowers	£ _____	£ _____
Equipment (tables, chairs)	£ _____	£ _____
Services (waiters, valet)	£ _____	£ _____

	Estimated Cost	Actual Cost
Other	£ _____	£ _____
Total	£ _____	£ _____
PHOTOGRAPHY/VIDEO		
Photographer	£ _____	£ _____
Videographer	£ _____	£ _____
Parents' album	£ _____	£ _____
Additional albums	£ _____	£ _____
Other	£ _____	£ _____
Total	£ _____	£ _____
HONEYMOON	£ _____	£ _____
Travel	£ _____	£ _____
Accommodation	£ _____	£ _____
Passports/visas	£ _____	£ _____
Vaccinations	£ _____	£ _____
Other	£ _____	£ _____
Total	£ _____	£ _____
ADDITIONAL	£ _____	£ _____
Gifts for bridal party	£ _____	£ _____
Bridesmaid's/flower girl's clothes	£ _____	£ _____
Transportation	£ _____	£ _____
Wedding night accommodation	£ _____	£ _____
Other	£ _____	£ _____
Total	£ _____	£ _____
TOTAL EXPENSES		
Engagement	£ _____	£ _____
Stationery	£ _____	£ _____
Bride's clothes	£ _____	£ _____
Groom's clothes	£ _____	£ _____
Ceremony	£ _____	£ _____
Wedding reception	£ _____	£ _____
Photos & video	£ _____	£ _____
Honeymoon	£ _____	£ _____
Additional	£ _____	£ _____
Final Cost	£ _____	£ _____

5   WEDDING TRADITIONS

Many of the rituals you go through from the time you get engaged to the time you return from your honeymoon have been part of the wedding celebration for centuries — exchanging rings, giving gifts, tossing the garter and the honeymoon. All of these are ancient customs which have been handed down from generation to generation.

Finding out where these customs came from and maybe including some of them in your wedding can add extra meaning to your celebration. Some of the customs long regarded as Irish are actually shared by many cultures and peoples.

BELIEFS AND SUPERSTITIONS

Probably the first tradition you participate in is the giving and receiving of an engagement ring. This can be dated back to ancient times, but it was the Egyptians who initiated the tradition which most resembles our own. In those days, a man gave his beloved something valuable, usually a gold coin, as a sign of his desire to marry her. If she accepted his gift, it signified to others their pledge to be married. Today, the coin has become a ring — an unending circle that symbolises the bond of true love.

In the early 1900s in Ireland, a couple would walk to church together on their wedding day. If the people of their parish approved of their union they would throw rice, pots, pans, brushes and other household goods at the couple. Today, hen parties (also called bridal showers) help a couple set up their new home.

Something old
Something new
Something borrowed
Something blue

This Victorian rhyme symbolises the ideals a bride desires for her new life. Nowadays, a piece of jewellery or other heirloom given to the bride by her mother often stands for 'something old', and is meant to symbolise the joy and love the bride brings to her future home. 'Something new' is usually the wedding dress or an accessory bought to wear on the day, and signifies the success she wishes for her husband and married life. 'Something borrowed' might be a handkerchief, veil or other trinket lent to the bride by a close friend or relative, and refers to the close friendships which she hopes to carry with her in her new life. And the 'something blue' is generally a blue garter, slip or ribbon sewn into the wedding dress. Blue is the colour of fidelity and symbolises the bride's commitment to her new relationship.

The fashionable or lucky colour for a bride's gown has changed constantly since the Middle Ages when red was all the rage in Europe. Irish brides considered blue to be very lucky: green was most unlucky — it was thought to be a temptation to the fairies to steal the bride away. In nineteenth-century France black was often worn. But it was the Victorians who introduced white as the colour of virginal purity and innocence and brides have been wearing white ever since.

Colour plays an important role in many countries still. In Mexico red beads are tossed at newly weds to bring them good luck, while Hindu brides wear a pink or red sari embroidered with gold. In many countries blue as in 'something blue' is worn — South African brides, for instance, wear a blue slip under their gown.

Although it is not clear where or when wearing a veil came from, it is known that it began as a symbol of modesty. In America the veil became popular when Nelly Curtis married President George Washington's aide, Major Lawrence Lewis. Apparently he became so enamoured of her after catching sight of her through a lace curtain that she decided to wear a veil on her wedding day.

A trousseau (from a French word meaning 'bundle') referred to the bundle of clothes and linens a bride would need to furnish her new home. Women from the bride's village would help her to weave and sew goods for her future home. Later these items would become part of her dowry, which was believed to enhance the value of an unmarried woman.

In the early 1900s, an Irish groom often paid 'luck money' to the family of the bride in order to bring happiness and blessings upon them. Then too, the dowry was paid by the bride's parents and was known as the 'bride's fortune'. On average it came to about £100 — a huge amount in those days.

Most couples are familiar with the superstition that the groom must never see his future wife in her gown before the ceremony, nor should she see herself in a mirror in full regalia. Both superstitions originated in the belief that marriage marks a break between an old life and a new one and that the two should never overlap. If the bride caught sight of herself in the mirror, she was believed to leave some of herself behind in the reflection. If the groom did see her in her dress, the wedding was generally postponed for a year!

Cakes have been part of weddings since Roman times when sweet cakes were believed to bring fertility, abundance and happiness. In ancient Rome, loaves of wheat bread were broken over the bride's head, eager guests ran to collect the crumbs which they believed would bring them good luck. Rice, long regarded in the Orient as a fertility symbol, was tossed at bridal couples long before confetti. In other cultures today, something small, traditionally a ring or coin, is baked into sweet cakes and passed around the bridal shower. Whoever finds the prize in her cake is believed to be the next to the altar. Wheat can also be incorporated into flower arrangements, or rice and wheat can be cooked into baked sweets and served to guests at the reception.

Tossing the garter and bridal bouquet had, and still has, everything to do with luck. Whoever catches the bouquet is thought to be lucky and is supposed to be the next woman to get married. In fourteenth-century France, the garter was considered particularly lucky and when it was tossed guests raced to claim it. Nowadays, the groom removes the garter from the bride's leg during the reception and tosses it to the single men: whichever of them catches it is believed to be the next to marry.

Some days of the week are believed to be luckier than others for a wedding: Monday for health, Tuesday for wealth, Wednesday the best day of all, Thursday for losses, Friday for crosses and Saturday no day at all, according to the old saying. It used to be forbidden to marry during Lent as this was a time of penance and preparation for Easter, but Shrove Tuesday and St Patrick's Day were considered the luckiest days to wed. The most unlucky day of the year was Good Friday. Even the months have superstitions attached, as the following poem sets out:

Marry when the year is new,	They who in July do wed,
Always loving, kind and true.	Must labour always for their bread.
When February birds do mate,	Whoever wed in August be,
You may wed, nor dread your fate.	Many a change are sure to see.
If you wed when March winds blow,	Marry in September's shine,
Joy and sorrow both you'll know.	Your living will be rich and fine.
Marry in April when you can,	If in October you do marry,
Joy for maiden and for man.	Love will come but riches tarry.
Marry in the month of May,	If you wed in bleak November,
You will surely rue the day.	Only joy will come, remember.
Marry when June roses blow,	When December's showers fall fast,
Over land and sea you'll go.	Marry and true love will last.

Honeymoons are thought to have originated from the days when couples married under a full moon and drank honeyed wine for thirty days, or until the moon waned. *Mí na meala* (or month of honey) the Irish word for 'honeymoon' also reflects this custom. Another tradition was that the couple went into hiding after the ceremony in case the bride's family tried to claim her back.

Carrying the bride over the threshold is an old Roman custom. The threshold was considered the domain of evil spirits who wanted to whisk the virgin bride away. A groom, wanting to keep his new wife, would carry her over the threshold so as to keep the spirits at bay.

An old French custom focuses on marriage as the alliance of two families, and celebrates this union with wine. During the reception the couple each raise a glass of wine from two different vineyards. They then pour their wine into one new glass and each of them drinks from it.

A lovely Belgian custom joins the families through flowers. As she walks up the aisle the bride stops and hands her mother a flower from her bouquet, and they embrace. During the recessional, the couple walks to the groom's side of the church and the bride gives her mother-in-law a second flower and they also embrace.

The Italians take a pragmatic view of marriage — five sugar-coated almonds representing the bitter and sweet sides of married life, are presented to guests. They stand for health, wealth, long life, fertility and happiness.

A Spanish groom gives his bride thirteen coins in memory of Christ and the twelve apostles. The bride carries them in a small bag during the ceremony as a symbol that the groom promises to support and care for her.

In Bermuda, couples plant a sapling in their garden on their wedding day to symbolise new beginnings. In other countries a red rose bush signifies a couple's growing love for each other.

STARTING YOUR OWN TRADITIONS

After all these ancient customs, why not initiate a new, totally personal tradition? This needn't cost anything, except a little time and imagination.

Have your wedding videotaped so that you can remember the day on anniversaries and other special occasions. Or keep a diary from the time you get engaged until after the honeymoon: in later years, you will enjoy reading it.

A lucky penny in your shoe can later be turned into a piece of jewellery. Ask a jeweller to make it into a pendant or ring setting or even a charm for a bracelet.

Buy special wine glasses to use on the day and then toast yourselves with them on special occasions in the years to come.

A French tradition has the bride and groom drinking from a *coupe de mariage* (a silver cup). Improvise by using a crystal or pewter cup engraved with your initials and wedding date: it can then be passed on through your family.

By ordering an extra case of the wine served on your wedding day, you can refill your wine glasses year after year to toast your anniversary.

A favourite wedding photograph can easily be turned into a Christmas ornament. As your own family grows, continue to add to your collection!

Be different and ask your groomsmen and bridesmaids to walk up the aisle together at the beginning of the ceremony. Or borrow an American tradition and let the groom, best man and other groomsmen walk up the aisle alone, followed by the bridesmaids and lastly the bride and her father.

Incorporate the Sign of Peace — a handshake or kiss — if you are having a church ceremony: walk among your guests and attendants.

Light a marriage candle during the ceremony, and relight it on each anniversary.

After the wedding, have your dress and veil cleaned and packed in acid-free tissue paper. You may want to offer it to your daughter to wear on her wedding day!

INCLUDING YOUR FAMILY

Another way to make your wedding unique is by involving family members and close relatives in your celebration. This is easy to do, and a few ideas follow. Don't forget to consult your celebrant when it has something to do with the ceremony.

– List your family members as 'honoured guests' on the first page of the Order of Service or Mass booklet.
– If someone has recently passed away or cannot be with you on the day, mention them in your Mass booklet or ask your celebrant to mention them briefly at the beginning of the ceremony.
– If you would like to make a more dramatic statement, place the absent person's favourite flowers somewhere others will see them possibly outside the entrance, in the inner hall or on the first pew. You could attach a little note to explain their importance.
– If a parent or family member has died recently, instead of tossing the bride's bouquet, keep the flowers to place on the grave.
– Ask a favourite niece or nephew to participate in the wedding as a flower girl, ring bearer, bridesmaid or usher.
– Invite your mothers to be part of the ceremony by bringing up the offertory.
– Bring talented family members to the fore — somebody might write a poem, sing or play a musical instrument for the ceremony or at the reception.
– Is there someone special who is not a part of the wedding party? Ask him or her to do a reading or recite a well-known poem.
– When a father walks his daughter down the aisle, it's a perfect time to share a special moment. Kiss him on the cheek and say something special.

- Ask your parents to take part in lighting the candles on either side of the unity candle. The two of you then take from your respective candles and light the centre one together — signifying the union of your families.
- After you have made your vows, invite your parents to reaffirm theirs.
- Have your photographer take a family portrait matching one that was taken when you and your brothers and sisters were children. Extra copies make lovely Christmas presents for family members.
- At the reception, make a special point of mentioning in the speeches your elderly relatives or those who made a special effort to be there.
- Invite both your parents to join you in the first dance, and encourage other family members to dance with you for the second dance.
- Be sure to reserve a special dance with your respective parents and in-laws.
- Honour your heritage by incorporating ethnic touches in your clothes, music, prayer, food or dance.
- Leave a special framed photo of your families on the guest book table at the reception. Better yet, leave family photo albums on the table for guests to peruse at their leisure. They'll enjoy seeing pictures of your parents or grandparents' weddings, and pictures of the two of you as youngsters.
- The bride might wear her mother's wedding dress, and the groom could wear his father's waistcoat. Carry a keepsake item that one of your parents had on their wedding day — a prayer book, special coin, pocket watch or bracelet.
- Take a few minutes before you leave the reception to thank your parents.

A Charm for Love

This is a charm I set for love; a woman's charm of love and desire;
a charm of God that none can break: You for me and I for thee and for none else;
your face to mine and your head turned away from all others.

Repeat three times secretly over a drink given to the beloved.

6 THE CEREMONY

Once you get engaged, it is easy to lose yourselves in pre-wedding activities. Parties, flowers, gifts and honeymoon plans can get in the way of what is really important on the day — the ceremony. Now is a good time to think about where you want to be married, by whom, and how. You may find yourself surprised by the answers.

Some people who would not have considered themselves very religious find that marriage brings out thoughts and feelings they had long since forgotten. Perhaps this is because weddings often renew emotional and family values in a person. On the other hand, some couples find they have moved away from their church and feel that to have a religious ceremony would be hypocritical. In this case, a registry office wedding or a marriage abroad might be appropriate.

Whatever you decide, keep in mind that this is your decision. Do not let well-intentioned family or friends chide you into a ceremony that you feel is not for you. If your parents expect a religious ceremony and become particularly upset, try to explain that you are not rejecting them or their beliefs. In the end of the day a marriage is the same — a union of two people who love each other and hope to spend their lives together — no matter where it is celebrated.

LEGAL REQUIREMENTS FOR MARRIAGE

Marriage in Ireland is a constitutionally valued institution and the law confers unique rights and obligations on the parties. In consequence, all couples are required by law to adhere to certain conditions before they wed. Specifically, both parties must be sixteen years of age or older, not already validly married, not related by blood or marriage, and of the opposite sex. The marriage of two persons, either of whom is under sixteen, is not valid unless permission has been granted by the president of the High Court or another High Court judge nominated by him. If either party is under twenty-one the consent of that person's parents or guardian will be required. The law prohibits marriage between certain individuals related by blood (both whole blooded relations and half blooded) or marriage. You may find it interesting to know that the following marriages are prohibited.

A man may not marry his:	*A woman may not marry her:*
Grandmother	Grandfather
Grandfather's wife	Grandmother's husband
Wife's grandmother	Husband's grandfather
Father's sister	Father's brother
Mother's sister	Mother's brother
Father's brother's wife	Father's sister's husband
Mother's brother's wife	Mother's sister's husband
Wife's father's sister	Husband's father's brother
Wife's mother's sister	Husband's mother's brother
Mother	Father
Stepmother	Stepfather
Wife's mother	Husband's father
Daughter	Son
Wife's daughter	Husband's son
Son's wife	Daughter's husband
Sister	Brother
Son's daughter	Son's son
Daughter's daughter	Daughter's son
Son's son's wife	Son's daughter's husband
Daughter's son's wife	Daughter's daughter's husband
Wife's son's daughter	Husband's son's son
Wife's daughter's daughter	Husband's daughter's son
Brother's daughter	Brother's son
Sister's daughter	Sister's son
Brother's son's wife	Brother's daughter's husband
Sister's son's wife	Sister's daughter's husband
Wife's brother's daughter	Husband's brother's son
Wife's sister's daughter	Husband's sister's son

WEDDING CEREMONIES

Most wedding ceremonies consist of two basic parts: the exchange of vows and the exchange of rings. Following is a brief overview of what is involved in various religious and civil marriage celebrations. This is by no means meant to cover all the details. It will, however, give you an idea of what to expect. The celebrant solemnising your marriage will be able to assist you further.

CATHOLIC MARRIAGE

Marriage is a sacrament in the Catholic Church and usually takes place within a Mass in the parish of the bride or her family. Couples must contact their priest at least three to six months in advance of their wedding date. This period of waiting is to give them ample time to consider and understand the importance of matrimony.

On rare ocasions a couple will be denied the right to marry in the church. This can happen if a priest feels one or both of the parties shows signs of serious immaturity or physical or mental instability. In the few times this does arise, the priest writes a report which is sent to the Chancellor. A new priest is asked to interview the couple and a second report is written. Based on the interviews and reports, the Chancellor makes a final decision, at which time the couple is advised.

Assuming permission is granted, banns may be posted in the church bulletin or read at church on three successive Sundays or Holy Days, and most couples will have to attend a pre-marriage course. (Your parish priest will advise you.)

CATHOLIC PRE-MARRIAGE COURSE

Pre-marriage courses are organised by the Catholic Marriage Advisory Council (CMAC) and are offered to assist couples in both the practical and spiritual aspects of marriage. The classes are run by lay people who are themselves married and trained in pre-marriage counselling. Discussions centre on marriage with relation to single life, love, potential problems, money, sexuality, and religion. A priest also attends the course but his input is generally directed at the spiritual aspects of marriage. There is no pressure to participate actively in a session, but by doing so you may be surprised to find that you enjoy the class and learn something new.

Typically the course is organised as five, two-hour sessions although a weekend course is also available. In exceptional cases, private one-to-one courses can be arranged through your priest.

DOCUMENTS

There are several documents you will need in order to be married in the Catholic Church.

1. Baptismal Certificate: A recent copy of your Baptismal Certificate (issued not more than six months before your wedding) is needed to prove that you have been baptised in a Christian faith thus allowing you to participate in the sacrament of marriage. You can obtain a copy of your certificate from the parish in which you were baptised.

2. *Pre-Nuptial Enquiry:* Basically this is an application for marriage. It takes no more than thirty minutes to complete and your priest will help you to fill it out. You will be asked if you understand the principles of a Christian marriage and if you are entering this relationship freely and willingly.

3. *Letter of Freedom:* If you have lived outside the parish in which you wish to marry for more than six months since the time you were sixteen, you will have to obtain a Letter of Freedom from the priest of the other parish in which you lived. This document declares that you are indeed free to marry at this time.

4. *Nihil Obstat:* When a marriage involves a foreign national, the Church requires a document saying the foreign national has not been married previously. Your priest can advise in more detail on this.

CEREMONY

A Catholic marriage requires two witnesses, usually the chief bridesmaid and best man, who also sign the register towards the end of the ceremony. The marriage can be celebrated as part of a full Mass or it may be carried out on its own. The latter is usually the case when one of you is not a Christian or has not been baptised.

If you are unsure as to which ceremony you would prefer, ask your priest for a copy of the service: take it home and the two of you can read it together. Once you have read it thoroughly, make a second appointment with your priest to discuss your preferences. Do not hesitate to ask about deleting or adding certain elements. Most priests are delighted when a couple takes a personal interest in their ceremony, and are willing to comply within reason.

One way to make your wedding more personal is through the readings which usually relate to love and marriage. Generally, there are two or three readings: one from the Old Testament and two from the New Testament, one of these being from one of the Gospels. The first two can be read by a close friend or relative who is not acting as a bridesmaid or groomsman.

You may wish to consider one of the following for your own

ceremony. If you need more assistance or are having trouble understanding their content, ask your priest for help:

OLD TESTAMENT READINGS	NEW TESTAMENT READINGS	GOSPEL READINGS
Genesis 1:25-31	Romans 13:8-10	John 2:1-11
Genesis 2:18-24	Ephesians 5:22-33	John 15:9-17
Ecclesiastes 3:1-14	1 Corinthians 11:1-12	Mark 10:6-9
Ecclesiastes 4:9-12	1 Corinthians 13:1-13	John 17:20-26
Ruth 1:16-17	Colossians 3:12-17	
Proverbs 31:10-31		

An offering is usually made to the parish, to the sacristan who prepares the church, to the altar boys and the organist. How much you give is a personal decision. If you are at all unsure, ask your priest what the average offering is and give more or less depending on your circumstances. To make things easy on the day, put the offerings in separate envelopes sealed and clearly labelled. Ideally this should be done the night before the wedding and given to your best man who can then make the offerings immediately following the cermony.

PAPAL BLESSING

A Papal Blessing is a certificate, signed by an official in Rome on behalf of the Pope, which blesses your marriage in the Catholic Church. Papal Blesssings come in several different designs and can be bought in religious bookshops such as Veritas. If you want to have it on the day, be sure to order the blessing at least three months in advance.

MARRIAGE IN THE CHURCH OF IRELAND

In the Church of Ireland, Holy Matrimony is a lifelong commitment in which a man and woman give themselves to each other in love, in the presence of God. Couples should contact their rector as soon as they decide to marry. He or she will go through the Service in detail, make suggestions about marriage preparation, reserve the church, and help you to fulfil one of the following legal requirements.

1. Banns of Marriage: For a couple to marry by publication of banns both parties must be Protestant Episcopalians (meaning a member of the Church of Ireland, the Church of England, the Episcopal Church of Scotland or any other Protestant Episcopal Church) and be resident in the parish for a minimum of three months. Banns must be read on three consecutive Sundays or Feast Days preceding the marriage, and the ceremony must take place in the church in which the banns have been read. If the two of you are from different parishes the banns must be read in both churches, and the clergy in whose church the marriage is not being solemnised must provide a certificate stating that the banns have been read and no objections have been made.

2. *Ordinary Licence:* An ordinary licence of marriage can be granted by any person (known as the licensor) nominated to do so by the Bishop. To be granted an ordinary licence one of the parties must be Protestant Episcopalian and must reside in the district of the parish where the marriage is to be celebrated for not less than seven days prior to making the application, or be an accustomed member of the parish for not less than three months. If neither party resides in the district of the church in which they wish to marry, their parish minister(s) must provide written consent to their marriage in the church they have selected. The above information must be given to the licensor in person or in writing. Both individuals must be over the age of twenty-one. If not, parental consent is required. After seven days of having given notice, an oath is taken or a declaration made and the licence may be granted and the marriage can then take place. A licence is only valid for three months.

3. *Special Licence:* Only a Bishop of the Church of Ireland may grant a special licence of marriage which allows couples to marry at any convenient place or time within the Bishop's jurisdiction. To be granted such a licence one of the parties must be a Protestant Episcopalian. The minister celebrating the marriage usually assists the couple in preparing a registrar's certificate which essentially outlines their particulars (name, date of birth, current marital status, current and future residence) and date and place of intended marriage. Otherwise, either party is required to acquire, complete, and return the certificate which can be obtained from the registrar of the district in which the marriage is to be celebrated.

There are two versions of the Church of Ireland marriage ceremony. The first is taken from the 1662 Book of Common Prayer and is traditional in wording. A second, introduced in 1987, is modern. If you are unfamiliar with either version, copies can be purchased at most religious bookstores.

JEWISH WEDDINGS

There are three major affiliates to the Jewish faith — Orthodox, Conservative and Reformed — and the marriage ceremony varies depending on which affiliation you belong to. All Jewish weddings, however, are both civil and religious in nature. For the Chief Rabbi's personal blessing that a wedding may proceed, a meeting needs to be set up between the bride, groom and the Rabbi, and a special form pertaining to the couple's status in Halach (Jewish law) must be completed.

Unlike many other religions, a Jewish wedding ceremony can take place in the open air, although in communities outside the land of Israel most are held in a synagogue. It can be performed any day except on Sabbath or Festivals, and certain periods of national mourning. If one member of the couple is not Jewish from birth, you will need to provide some proof of your Orthodox conversion before the marriage can take place under the Chief Rabbinate of Ireland.

Clothes for a mainstream Orthodox, Conservative or Reform wedding are conventional. The bride usually wears white and the groom wears a tuxedo or dark suit. All men attending an Orthodox or Conservative ceremony wear skullcaps or hats, which are furnished by the synagogue for guests who do not have them.

The ceremony is preceded by the singing of various psalms followed by traditional chants greeting the bride and groom. The marriage itself takes place under a Chuppah, or wedding canopy, which is open on all four sides. This is to signify that the home the couple are establishing should be accessible to all — family, friends and strangers, all who care to enter from the four points of the compass. The Chuppah is made of fabric and is usually ornamented. Alternatively, a tallit (prayer shawl) may be held just above the couple's head by four men.

At the start of the ceremony, the couple is escorted to the canopy by both sets of parents, bridesmaids and groomsmen. The bride stands to the right of the groom. Parents, bridesmaids and groomsmen stand around the couple. The actual ceremony varies depending on your affiliation. When you meet with your Rabbi, you should go through the ceremony together and talk about ways to add a personal touch.

At the conclusion of the ceremony, the groom crushes a glass, wrapped in a napkin. This is to remind us that even in the midst of joy, our Temple in Jerusalem remains in ruins. Once the glass is broken, everyone present wishes the couple 'Mazel tov', or good luck.

MORMON WEDDINGS

The Church of Latter Day Saints recognises two types of wedding celebration. The first is a civil ceremony, performed in Ireland by the couple's Branch President, the local priesthood leader, or Bishop. The second ceremony, held in the temple, is for members who meet particular requirements closely held by the church. As there are no temples in Ireland, Irish couples must travel to London for this special ceremony.

Couples wishing to be married in the Mormon Church must first start by contacting their Branch President or Bishop soon after their engagement is announced. Your Branch President will offer guidance as you plan the ceremony and will assist in the completion of registry documents required by the State.

Once all the necessary paperwork is complete the civil ceremony may take place in your local chapel. A Mormon wedding requires two witnesses, for example the chief bridesmaid and best man, neither of whom has to be Mormon. If you prefer, however, other witnesses may be selected. Guests of all religions are welcome to attend. No photographs may be taken inside the chapel, but they may be taken in other parts of the building.

Similarly, photographs are not allowed inside the temple. This is to keep the service as sacred as possible. Couples wanting a temple service, and who are in good standing in the church, should make arrangements through their Branch President. It is during this celebration that Mormon marriages are sealed 'for time and eternity'. Non-Mormons are not allowed to witness the service but are welcome guests at the reception.

QUAKER MARRIAGES

A Quaker wedding is a Christian marriage recognised by both Church and State as legally binding. The ceremony itself is a simple, quiet affair taking place on a weekday in a Meeting House, either at a usual Meeting for Worship or at a Meeting specially arranged for the marriage. Couples marrying in the Religious Society of Friends take their spouses with the promise to be a faithful and loving partner for as long as they both shall live.

For your marriage to take place you must first apply to the clerk(s) of your respective Monthly Meeting(s) who will detail the procedure and assist you in filling out the necessary paperwork. Because a Quaker marriage is both a religious and civil ceremony, requirements of both must be satisfied. Therefore a couple must obtain either a Special Licence or a Registrar's Certificate before the marriage can take place. As regards the Meeting House in which the marriage is to be solemnised, arrangements should be made with the Monthly Meeting Clerk.

Registrar's Certificate: Your Monthly Meeting Clerk will advise you about obtaining this. Once the registrar's certificate has been issued it must be presented to the Clerk of the Liberating Monthly Meeting, which is normally the woman's Monthly Meeting, though when only the man is in membership it is the monthly meeting of the Meeting House in which the marriage is to take place.

Special Licence: If the regulations regarding period of residence cannot be complied with, the Clerk of the Yearly Meeting may issue a Special Licence. To be granted such a licence, one of the parties must be a Member, and a Registrar's Certificate is not necessary prior to marriage, but a State Certificate (which can be obtained from the Monthly Meeting) must be completed on solemnisation of the marriage. Later the State Certificate is forwarded to the State Registrar of the district in which the marriage took place.

In the presence of local Friends and specially invited guests, you will take your vows. Normally at the beginning of the Meeting for Worship for the solemnisation of the marriage a Friend will explain the procedure. During the Meeting, when the couple feels the time is right, they stand, join hands and in the presence of God and the congregation, make their declaration. Wedding rings may be exchanged if desired. The Meeting continues, and the Quaker marriage certificate, having been signed by the couple and two witnesses, is read aloud by the Registering Officer of the Society of Friends. The Meeting is ended in due course by the Elders shaking hands. Immediately following, the State Marriage Certificate is signed by the couple and all present are invited to sign the Quaker Marriage Certificate.

For further details on Quaker marriage, please consult the Book of Discipline or the Clerk or Record Clerk of the Monthly Meeting.

INTERFAITH MARRIAGE

An interfaith marriage can sometimes present special problems, but talking to your clergy can be of some help. Nowadays, church weddings are possible as many clergy are willing to marry couples of different religions (except the Jewish faith). It may be possible to have both your ministers officiate at the ceremony. Generally, the service is performed in one religion and prayers are offered by the assisting clergy. You should talk through this possibility with the clergy presiding over your wedding.

If you are Catholic, marrying a baptised Christian, you need to request dispensation from the local Bishop in order to marry. You must also verbally promise to raise your children within the unity of the marriage in the Catholic faith. Some couples find this poses no problem. If it does, then the positive side is that the concerns have come to light before your wedding day. Take time to discuss your feelings on this with each other. If need be, consult your families and clergy.

One suggestion which might prove helpful is to attend a few services in each other's place of worship. This may give you a better sense of one another's faith and alleviate any first-time nerves which are better not experienced on your wedding day!

REGISTRY OFFICE MARRIAGE

A registry office wedding is a legally binding contract of marriage. Couples wanting to marry on the authority of the Registrar's Licence or Certificate may do so on completion of certain conditions. For either document to be issued, either party must serve notice of the intended marriage to the district registrar. If the individuals live in different districts, notice must be served to both registrars.

Notice of marriage contains the following information: parties' names, current marital status, profession, age, address, the place of worship either party regularly attends, and place of worship where the marriage is to be held. If neither party has been active in a particular faith for one month prior to serving the notice of marriage, a special notice will be inserted in a local newspaper. The registrar's office supplies the proper wording. Proof of the published notice is required prior to the wedding day. As mentioned, the certificate or licence may be required for a religious ceremony to take place.

Registrar's Licence: To be married on the authority of the Registrar's Licence one of the parties must swear in writing that both parties are free to marry, that one of them has been resident in the district in which they wish to marry for fourteen days, and if a place of worship is named, that they have been attending it for not less than one month. If either party is under the age of twenty-one, written consent from that person's parents will be necessary. On the fifteenth day, notice of the intended marriage may be served on the registrar either in person or in writing. Eight days after giving notice the registrar may grant a licence and the ceremony can then take place. A registrar's licence is valid for three months from the date of serving the notice.

Registrar's Certificate: Parties wishing to marry on the authority of the Registrar's Certificate must both be residents of the district in which they wish the marriage to take place for a period not less than seven days. Notice of the intended marriage must be served on the district registrar and for cases where the partners live in different districts, notice must be served on both registrars. On the twenty-second day after notice has been served, a certificate may be issued by the registrar and the wedding can take place. From the eighth day of serving notice, and after the twenty-second day, neither party need reside in Ireland. A registrar's certificate is valid for three months from the date of serving the notice.

Special Licence: A special licence may be granted in exceptional cases by the Registrar-General upon proof that one of you is unable for health reasons to participate in a ceremony at a registry office. If granted, the ceremony may be celebrated in any place and at any time by the registrar of your district.

When one or both of you has previously been married, you will need to supply either a Death Certificate or a Divorce Decree Absolute. In relation to a divorce, two questionnaires (given at the time of serving notice) will have to be filled out and returned by the parties involved in the divorce. These will then be forwarded to the Registrar-General whose permission must be given before the wedding ceremony can take place. The waiting period is only around two to three weeks.

The fee for a registrar wedding is £32.50 plus the cost of the newspaper ad, if needed. Weddings can take place during office hours. Each county in Ireland has at least one registry office, where you can get specific details of opening times. As in other weddings, two witnesses are needed for all registry office ceremonies.

WEDDINGS ABROAD

Perhaps the two of you have decided you would like to be married abroad. If so, you should be aware that your marriage will be recognised in Ireland so long as it is celebrated in accordance with the law of the country you are in and is in keeping with Ireland's strict law regarding monogamy. Should you already be abroad when you decide to get married, contact the Irish Embassy or Consul in your host country, to be sure that all necessary steps have been taken for your marriage to be legally recognised in Ireland.

There are several combination holidays which allow you to be married in one city and then travel to another for your honeymoon. One such example is a wedding in Rome.

Many couples travel to Rome every year to be married in the Irish College Church. If you have no contact there, you could write to the Rector, Pontificio Collegio Irlandese, Via Santi Quattro 1, 00184 Roma, Italy, or telephone from Ireland at 00-396-731-5697.

Planning such a wedding requires a minimum of three months preparation, the assistance of your parish priest , and the completion of several documents. In adddition to needing current Irish passports, the Italian authorities require written proof that you are free to marry. Your parish priest can organise Letters of Freedom (a letter declaring your freedom to marry), and the consular section at the Department of Foreign Affairs can assist you in preparing other documentation. The Department of Foreign Affairs is open Monday to Friday 10:00-12:30 and 2:30-4:00, telephone 01-4780822.

Contact your travel agent for more detailed information about foreign wedding destinations. For the best value, telephone three or four agents and compare prices and packages.

> *Marriage was a rather casual affair in sixteenth-century Ireland under the Brehon laws when Granuaile married Iron Dick Burke for a period of 'one year certain', meaning that either party could withdraw after a year if they so wished.*

CEREMONY PLANNER

Fill in the details of your wedding ceremony here:

Date of ceremony _____ Time _____
Officiant _____ Tel. _____
Address _____
_____
_____

Pre-marriage course information _____
_____
_____

Documents needed _____
_____
_____

Date of Banns/public notice _____
_____

Selected readings/prayers _____
_____
_____
_____
_____
_____

NOTES

7 VISION OF BEAUTY

What makes a bride really beautiful on her wedding day? It is a combination of things, the first of which is happiness. No amount of skilfully applied make-up can bring that radiance to your face quite the way real happiness does. Even so, if you don't take good care of yourself in the weeks and months leading up to the big day, you may not look your best. Regular exercise, good diet and plenty of sleep are just as important as finding the right nail varnish or the perfect lipstick. And finally, a beautiful dress and accessories will give the finishing touch and make you a vision of beauty on your wedding day.

THE PERFECT DRESS

No matter what style of wedding you are planning, start the hunt for that perfect dress at least four to six months before the day. This allows plenty of time to order or design and make alterations. Look in the *Golden Pages* under 'Bridal Shops', 'Dress-Suit Hire' and 'Dress Manufacturing', or ask friends for their recommendations.

Before you begin, think about your wedding carefully. The type of dress you choose will be determined by your overall style — which is somewhat determined by the time of day the ceremony takes place — and your budget. Before going into detail about the various styles and how to personalise them, lets explain a few fashion terms first.

FASHIONS AND FABRIC

Knowing these terms will help you express your ideas clearly to dressmakers or shop assistants.

A-Line: Skirt with close-fitting waist and flared hemline.

Antebellum: Waistline of skirt falls naturally to waist but comes to a point in the centre front.

Ballerina skirt: Full skirt that falls to ankles.

Basque waistline: Long waist that falls about two inches below natural waistline and may come to a point in centre front, also known as dropped waist.

Batiste: Fine, thin fabric often made of cotton or rayon, etc.

Bell sleeve: Long sleeve that flares gently from below shoulder to wrist.

Bodice: Upper part of gown.

Bolero: Short jacket to waist, without collar and often without buttons, usually worn open.

Bouffant: Full gathered veil, usually worn towards back of head, creating a halo effect.

Brocade: Ornamental fabric woven with raised design.

Brush Train: Short train that barely brushes the floor.

Bugle Beads: Tiny tubular beads used as decoration.

Bustle: Gathering of train on waistline at back of gown which allows ease of movement.

Cap sleeve: Short sleeve that covers top of arm, usually unfitted.

Cathedral train: Train extending approximately three yards from waistline.

Chapel train: Train extending one and one-third yards from waistline.

Chintz: Cotton fabric, usually glazed, either plain or with printed pattern.

Court train: Train extending one yard from waistline.

Crepe: Thin, crinkled fabric made of cotton, rayon, etc.

Dolman sleeve: Long sleeve that starts wide at shoulder and narrows down to wrist.

Face veil: Short veil that covers the face, usually worn at beginning of ceremony.

Fitted bodice: Tight-fitting top.

Fitted sleeve: Long sleeve, tight from shoulder to wrist.

Floor length: Skirt that falls to one inch above floor.

Full skirt: Skirt gathered at waistline to create bouffant effect.

Juliet cap: Fitted cap worn at back of head.

Leg-of-mutton sleeve: Bouffant shoulder leading towards wrist in more fitted form.

Midriff: Part of gown from just below bust to waistline.

Moiré: Fabric, usually made from silk, characterised by wavy or watermark pattern, also known as taffeta.

Organza: Sheer silk or synthetic fabric.

Point sleeve: Long sleeve that comes to a point over back of hand.

Raw silk: Rough textured natural silk.

Royal train: Longest train, extending three yards or more from waistline.

Satin: Smooth, glossy fabric made of silk, rayon, or nylon.

Sequin: Small, shiny decoration sewn onto fabric for sparkling effect.

Train: Fabric, matching gown, that trails behind dress.

Tulle: Fine netting used for veils and sheer panels on gown.

Waistline: Narrowest part of waist.

STYLE

The style of your dress will be somewhat dictated by the time of day your ceremony takes place. This is particularly true for an ultra-formal or formal celebration. Although a short dress with a train is very chic for example, it is not appropriate on these occasions. A few pointers on style follow.

Ultra-formal or formal day-time: Champagne, ivory, cream or white floor-length dress with a brush or court train; a matching long veil and face veil; simple jewellery, pearls are ideal.

Personal touches: Wear two or three lengths of veil or a Juliet cap with a long veil attached, or consider a floral wreath and veil; gloves are very elegant with short sleeves; dried flowers sewn to the bodice are unusual and quite striking.

Ultra-formal or formal evening: Champagne, ivory, cream or white floor-length dress with a chapel or cathedral train. Fabric and lace can be more ornamental than the formal day-time dress; a long veil extending the length of the train; simple jewellery.

Personal touches: As for formal day-time.

Semi-formal day-time/evening: Champagne, ivory, cream, white or pastel dress in a variety of lengths from floor to ballerina-length, fabrics for evening are more ornamental; bouffant, elbow or shoulder length evening veil; gloves are an option; jewellery simple.

Personal touches: If the dress is floor length, a court train is appropriate but optional: if the dress is shorter, a long train can be attached and is rather stylish.

Informal day/evening: Any stylish day dress or suit is appropriate as are ballerina-length dresses.

Personal touches: A short veil or hat with netting is lovely.

Take magazine clippings of dresses you like with you when you visit a dressmaker or start your shopping. Ask about alterations before you order as these costs can add up. And, when possible, get a picture of yourself in the dress for reference when buying other accessories.

BUYING, HIRING, MAKING

Next you need to decide whether you want to buy, hire or have your wedding dress made. Buying your dress is perhaps the ideal. But, unfortunately, your wedding dress is probably the most expensive dress you will ever buy — particularly when you consider that it is worn only once. If you plan well ahead of time, you should be able to find a few bargains as many dresses go on sale out of season. A less expensive option is to buy a secondhand dress and make alterations. Many secondhand dresses are just as lovely as new ones and can be revamped by changing buttons or lace or by adding a train or decoration.

Hiring or borrowing a dress is a great alternative if you do not want to spend money on an expensive dress but do want the traditional look on your wedding day. If you hire a dress, be sure to check whether you can collect it the day before the wedding and whether it must be dry cleaned before returning. If a friend lends you her dress, don't make any changes to it without asking first! After your wedding, ask your bridesmaid to have the dress cleaned and properly packed while you are on honeymoon before returning it.

Having your dress made or making it yourself creates a genuine one-of-a-kind dress. Don't attempt to make your own dress unless you are an accomplished seamstress. Even then make a dummy model first out of less expensive material so you can see the results and alter it if necessary before beginning on the real dress.

 If you cannot sew, don't worry. Professional dressmakers are easily found. You may have a good friend or relative who is a seamstress and would be willing to help you or even make your dress for you. Try to provide a pattern or pictures of the dress you want and discuss ideas with the designer — you want to be happy with the result!

CROWNING GLORY

Start looking for a headpiece or veil once you have decided on a wedding dress. Today, the choices seem infinite, ranging from traditional sweeping veils as long as cathedral trains to chic pillbox hats with a hint of netting. Just remember, the headpiece should complement, not overpower you.

JULIET CAP   PILLBOX   BOUFFANT

WREATH   TIARA

Make sure your headpiece matches the colour of your dress exactly and is of the same or complementary fabric. Lace and tulle are popular choices. Your headpiece should also flatter your face and hairstyle. Tall women with oval faces are lucky and can usually wear any style. Women with rounder faces may wish to elongate their look by wearing a tiara. And a floral headpiece or a bouffant veil can soften a long face.

If you are wearing a smart suit rather than a long dress, or if you prefer a more natural look, try a wreath of flowers or elegant velvet headband. Pretty combs or ribbons are simple alternatives which look lovely with either an informal or a traditional wedding dress. When you are making your decision, consider these tips:

– Take along a photo of your dress when shopping.
– If possible wear your hair the way you plan to on your wedding day.
– Wear a top with a neckline shaped like that of your wedding dress.
– Ask a close friend or relative to go shopping with you — an honest second opinion is always helpful.
– Find a headpiece with a detachable veil — you'll be glad you did during the reception.

ACCESSORIES

Buy your underwear and accessories only after you have selected your dress. Lingerie should be white or a soft pastel colour so it does not show through your clothes. As soon as possible, try everything on with your dress and check the front, back, sides and shoulders to make sure nothing shows through in a standing, sitting, kneeling or dancing position.

Shoes should be bought, covered or dyed to match the dress. If covering shoes, buy light-coloured, comfortable shoes and supply the fabric to match your dress. Raw silk or synthetic materials make beautiful wedding-day shoes. The height of the heel is strictly up to you but keep in mind that you will be wearing these shoes all day and comfort is important. If the shoes are new, wear them a few times before the big day to break them in — be sure to scuff the bottoms so they do not slip or slide.

Many a bride and bridesmaid have laddered their stockings on the morning of the wedding. Have a second pair of tights for the female members of the bridal party.

Keep your jewellery to a minimum so that it doesn't detract from your dress and veil. A simple pendant, string of pearls or gold chain are ideal. Generally, a watch is not worn by the bride on her wedding day as it is not a day to be concerned about time! If you have an engagement ring, wear it on your right hand during the ceremony so that your wedding ring can be slipped on your left hand easily. If your engagement ring locks into the wedding band, give it to your partner the night before the ceremony, and check that the best man knows he should have both on the day.

At the end of this chapter you will find a bride's organiser to help you keep track of your wedding clothes details.

BRIDAL BEAUTY

The big day is just around the corner and you are exhausted! Too late to learn that the month before the wedding is not the time to start taking care of yourself. To look your best on your wedding day, plan a beauty schedule at least two months beforehand which includes exercise, eating well and plenty of sleep. If you want to lose a few pounds, consult a doctor or dietitian as soon as possible for a sensible and balanced diet. It may sound excessive, but work out what day in your menstrual cycle your wedding falls on — the last thing you want is to be suffering from pre-menstrual tension or to be having your period on your wedding day. If you have any concerns, consult your doctor or clinic for advice.

Exercise: Take time to exercise at least three times a week for not less than twenty minutes. Aerobics, jogging, swimming, tennis or even walking not only burns calories but reduces stress.

Start slowly. Take five minutes to warm up and another five minutes at the end of each workout to cool down. Mix routines so you don't get bored or overwork any one muscle group. In the few weeks leading up to the wedding day, avoid stressful exercise — you don't want an aching or sore muscle on your wedding day.

Eat well: A regular, balanced diet should keep you healthy. Stress causes some people to eat more than normal, so keep high calorie foods out of the house in the weeks before the wedding. Don't be too strict with your diet — a treat every now and then won't do any harm.

Sleep: Stick to your bedtime ritual. If sleep evades you, get up and do something relaxing like reading or taking a bath. A long hot soak with bubbles, scented oils or herbs can ease tension away and also gives you some time to yourself. Fill the tub with warm water and add fresh lemon geranium, lavender, rose petals or rosemary sprigs for a soothing treat.

Lack of sleep can wreak havoc on your skin. To return that healthy glow, cleanse, exfoliate, tone and moisturise regularly. If you are not sure what products to use, consult a beautician. If your skin is particularly bothersome, talk to your chemist, or even see a dermatologist.

Everyone will want to see your rings on your wedding day so it is a good idea to show them off to advantage by having a manicure. This is relatively inexpensive, ranging from £5- £10. But if you would prefer to do your own nails, follow these easy steps:

MANICURE

- Soak your hands in warm soapy water for five minutes and loosen any dirt with a nail brush or orange stick.
- Dry your hands completely and shape your nails with a professional emery board, available at most chemists.

- Apply cream around each cuticle and gently push them back with a cotton-wrapped orange stick.
- Apply a base coat and two coats of nail varnish, wait a few minutes and apply a top coat.

PEDICURE

While you are doing your nails, why not complete your beauty regime with an at-home pedicure:

- Soak your feet for ten minutes in warm, sudsy water or plan on giving yourself a pedicure right after a long, relaxing bath. Using a wet pumice stone, gently rub away the dead rough skin from the soles of your feet.
- Dry your feet. With an orange stick and soft nailbrush, clean behind the nail and gently push back the cuticles.
- Clip the nails straight across and smooth the edges with an emery board. Don't file the sides as this can cause ingrown nails. Rinse feet and dry.
- Apply a moisturiser and massage into feet.
- Weave tissue or cotton between your toes and apply a base coat to the nails. Follow with two coats of coloured nail varnish and finally a top coat.
- For best results, let dry for at least twenty minutes and remain barefoot for one hour.

ATTENDANTS' DRESSES

Choose the bridesmaids' dresses at roughly the same time as your dress to allow for ordering or designing and alterations. The dresses should be similar in style to your dress and in a complementary colour.

To make things easy, pre-select two or three colours and styles and let the bridesmaids make the final decision. Nowadays, bridesmaids often pay for their own dresses, so naturally you will want to leave the final choice to them. If the dresses are very expensive or cannot be worn again, you or your family should offer to pay for all or part of the costs.

Your chief bridesmaid is usually someone very special to you. Ideally, her outfit should distinguish her from your other bridesmaids. Her dress might be different in colour or style, for example, or her bouquet might vary in shape and colour.

The flower girl's dress can be a scaled down version of the bridesmaids' or one that complements a wedding theme. Or follow an American tradition and dress her in a miniature version of your dress. At the end of this chapter you will find a planner for the bridesmaids' and flower girls' wedding clothes. Use it to keep everyone's details in one place.

ATTENDANTS' ACCESSORIES

A good rule of thumb for attendants' accessories is 'simple but elegant'. Shoes should complement or match the dress in fabric and colour. Stockings are best in a neutral or cream shade, and jewellery should not attract too much attention.

MOTHERS' DRESSES

In the months before the wedding both mothers might like to meet, maybe for lunch, and talk through their ideas. While their outfits should never be identical, they could be in keeping with one another. Ideally, complementary styles and colours or shades of the same colour look best and tie in with the overall wedding style.

The length of their dresses is largely determined by the formality and time of day at which the wedding takes place, as well as their own preferences. A formal evening wedding may call for a floor length or cocktail-style dress and can be heavily accessorised. For formal and semi-formal day-time weddings, ballerina-length dresses look best matched with shoes, gloves and handbags. For informal weddings a suit or dress with matching hat, gloves and shoes looks stylish.

Old folk remedy

To leave skin fair and clear, anoint with distilled water of walnuts — or with the blood of a bull or of a hare!

BRIDE'S ORGANISER

Here is a quick guide to items you may need on your wedding day:

CEREMONY	GOING AWAY	HONEYMOON
Curling tongs	Corsage flower	Accessories
Dress	Gloves	Hairdryer
Garter	Handbag	Camera
Gloves	Hat	Casual clothes
Jewellery	Jewellery	Curling tongs
Hairdryer	Make-up	Dressing gown
Make up	Outfit	Formal clothes
Nail varnish	Shoes	Jewellery
Lingerie	Slip	Lingerie
Penny for your shoe	Stockings/tights	Make-up
Shoes	Suspender belt	Medication
Slip	Lingerie	Money
Stockings/tights		Nail varnish
Suspender belt		Passport/Visa
Something Old		Shampoo/Soap
Something New		Shoes
Something Borrowed		Sportswear
Something Blue		Sweaters/Coat
Veil/headpiece		Swimsuit
		Reading material
		Walkman

WEDDING DRESS PLANNER

Dress maker/shop _____

Contact _____ Tel _____

Address _____

Colour/style _____

_____

_____

Fitting dates _____

_____

Fabric _____ Pattern _____

Cost £ _____ Deposit £ _____ Balance due £ _____

ATTENDANTS' PLANNER

Chief bridesmaid _____ Tel. _____

Address _____

Dress size _____ Bust _____ Hips _____

Length _____ Glove size _____ Shoe size _____

Fitting dates _____

Bridesmaid _____ Tel. _____

Address _____

Dress size _____ Bust _____ Hips _____

Length _____ Glove size _____ Shoe size _____

Fitting dates _____

Bridesmaid _____ Tel. _____

Address _____

Dress size _____ Bust _____ Hips _____

Length _____ Glove size _____ Shoe size _____

Fitting dates _____

Bridesmaid _____ Tel. _____

Address _____

Dress size _____ Bust _____ Hips _____

Length _____ Glove size _____ Shoe size _____

Fitting dates _____

Flower girl _____ Tel. _____

Address _____

Dress size _____ Bust _____ Hips _____

Length _____ Shoe size _____

Fitting dates _____

NOTES

8   THE LEADING MAN

The bride seems to be the focus of attention in the run up to a wedding. On the day itself though, make sure you provide the perfect match. Like your partner, getting plenty of exercise, rest and relaxation in the months beforehand will ensure you look your best. Then it is just a matter of deciding what you are going to wear!

This depends largely on how formal your wedding is to be, the colour scheme the bride has chosen for herself and her bridesmaids, and the time of day at which the wedding is to take place. Traditionally, the groom wears monochrome colours — a black tail jacket or morning coat, white collar, grey tie and waistcoat. Your accessories (tie, handkerchief and waistcoat) can be co-ordinated with those of your bride and the bridesmaids.

STYLE

It is customary for the men in the bridal party — fathers of the bride and groom, best man, groomsmen and ushers — to take their cue from you. And, like you, their wedding clothes should complement those worn by the bride and bridesmaids. If, for instance, the bridesmaids wear lilac, the groomsmen might wear toning ties, cummerbunds, handkerchiefs or buttonholes to give a co-ordinated look.

WHAT TO WEAR

Formal day-time:
  – *Traditional* — morning coat or tails in black or grey; striped trousers; grey waistcoat; white wing-collared shirt; silk grey cravat; and top hat, gloves and black shoes. For a touch of style, exchange the grey cravat for a striped or checked one. And when wearing a black morning coat, tuck a white silk

handkerchief into the breast pocket. (A bowtie is *never* worn.)

- *Modern* — as above but with white turndown collar shirt and grey silk tie rather than a cravat. Or be ultra chic with a bright brocade or patterned waistcoat. Another colour option is navy.
- Socks: black cotton or silk; shoes: black patent leather lace-ups; top hat and gloves to match or complement the morning coat.

Formal evening:

- *Traditional* — black evening tails; white Marcella waistcoat with matching bowtie; white wing-collared shirt with cuffs; black top hat, white gloves and silk handkerchief. (Generally, turndown collars are not worn with evening dress.)
- *Modern* — black evening dinner jacket (double breasted optional) and black evening trousers; white wing-collared shirt with cuffs; waistcoat or cummerbund with bowtie.
- Socks: black cotton or silk; shoes: black patent leather lace-up or slip-on; handkerchief, if desired, white or black silk in breast pocket; white scarf with hand knotted fringe.

Semi-formal day-time:

- *Traditional* — grey or black lounge jacket; striped morning trousers; grey waistcoat; white soft-collared shirt and tie. For a slightly different look, wear a striped or small check tie.
- *Modern* — double-breasted suit in subtle stripe; white wing-collared shirt; bow-tie; coloured or patterned pocket handkerchief.

Semi-formal evening:

- Single-breasted dinner jacket with silk facing; black trousers (stripe optional); white dress shirt; cummerbund and bowtie. In warm weather a white or ivory dinner jacket with black evening trousers looks classy.
- You may prefer to update this look with a double-breasted suit teamed with matching or contrasting trousers, and a bowtie to match the bridesmaids' dresses.
- Socks: black cotton or silk; shoes: black patent leather lace-up or slip-on.

Informal day/evening:

- Black, grey, charcoal, brown or navy suit (single or double-breasted). In summer, a white or natural shade of jacket and dark trousers, or a navy jacket worn with white trousers is very smart looking. Or try an elegant pinstripe suit.

If you are a member of the Army or Gardaí, you may want to wear your uniform. Likewise, if you are not Irish and feel more comfortable wearing the traditional wedding dress of your country, do so. Nothing is more dashing than a Scotsman in a kilt! Unless the wedding is a formal or semi-formal affair, there is no real need to buy a suit specially for the occasion.

ACCESSORIES

Not just for the bride anymore! Men, too, can exert their personality and show a little individuality by choosing from a range of accessories. Ties, cravats, bowties, waistcoats, handkerchiefs, pocketwatches, cummerbunds, socks, shirt studs and cuff links come in a huge variety of colours, textures and styles. So shop around until you find something you feel happy with — always keeping in mind the overall colour scheme of the bridal party.

On formal occasions, for instance, a silk bowtie is perfect but a patterned fabric, either in satin moiré or brocade finish, is more interesting. Brighten a black dinner jacket with a yellow print bowtie and a purple silk handkerchief. Rejuvenate a grey double-breasted evening jacket with a paisley bowtie and cummerbund. Fine patterns in vivid colours add sparkle to the most traditional suits. Match a polka dot bowtie and cummerbund with a white dinner jacket and black trousers for an up-to-the-minute look.

Knowing how to mix and match accessories is important in pulling a look together. A subtle touch of colour gives a groom a distinguished look, but do take care with items you don't often wear. When wearing a bowtie, for example, don't let the fittings (buckles, clips or elastic) show under the collar.

If you are wearing a waistcoat, several designs are available at men's clothes shops, dress suit hire shops, and department stores. Traditionally, waistcoats are cut in the same shade as or in a contrasting colour to the suit jacket but in the same fabric. Black and grey are popular. But, lately, more unusual waistcoats in satin, moiré or brocade are fashionable and can be made to match the bride or bridesmaids' dresses.

Shirts also come in a variety of designs and colours. Fronts range from plain to pleated to embroidered. Collars can be either wing or turndown. Cuffs should always be double. Dress studs are available in pearl, gold, black and faux stone and are more elegant than buttons. They should, however, be forgotten altogether when covered by a front fly (a fold in the shirt that covers the buttons).

The old world look of top hat and gloves adds an air of grace and charm to a wedding. However, many men today feel uncomfortable wearing them, even when their wedding is formal. If wearing a hat and gloves makes you feel self-conscious then don't bother — why feel ill at ease on your wedding day? If you enjoy the sense of occasion they lend, however, then wear them to arrive at the ceremony. Once there, remove hat and gloves and hold them in your left hand — leaving the other hand free to shake hands.

If all the men in your party are wearing top hat and gloves, you would be wise to write your name on a piece of masking tape and stick it to the inside of your hat, under the crease. So as not to lose your gloves, keep them in your hat.

HIRING

If you plan to hire a suit, order it at least six to eight weeks prior to the wedding. There is a wide range of suits to choose from and reputable dress hire shops will have knowledgeable staff and brochures to help you decide. An entire head to toe outfit can be hired. Normally, suits are hired out by the day but, if your wedding is on a Saturday, there is usually no charge for Sunday. If you cannot take the suit back yourself, ask your best man to do so promptly — late fees add up quickly.

GROOM'S DUTIES

These days there are no concrete rules about who organises or pays for what but, according to tradition, the groom is responsible for the rings, flowers for the bridal party and special guests, transport for himself and the best man to the ceremony and for himself and the bride to the reception, as well as gifts for the best man, groomsmen, ushers and bridesmaids. Turn to the end of the chapter for a month-by-month checklist of duties.

TRANSPORT

Transport to and from the ceremony and reception is one of those essential details which, with a little thought, can be turned into an imaginative, romantic or chic part of the wedding. In days gone by, couples used to walk to the ceremony together and then on to the reception. Today, Rolls Royces, horse-drawn carriages, fancy limousines, helicopters, buses or old-fashioned cars are all used.

As mentioned above, the groom is traditionally expected to pay for transport for himself and the best man to the ceremony and then for himself and the bride to the reception. If you want to spend less money and make things easier for everyone, ask the best man to drive you to the ceremony, hire a car to drive the bride and her father to the ceremony and use the same vehicle to take the two of you to the reception. If money is tight, ask a friend or relative to lend you a car for the day and decorate it with ribbons and streamers.

Others who may need transport on the day include the bride's mother — although she may wish to be driven by a relative or family friend — and the bridesmaids. If the bridesmaids dress at the bride's house, they can go to the ceremony in the same car as the bride and her father. Use the transport organiser at the end of this chapter to keep track of your transport needs.

FLOWERS

As a general rule, the bride takes care of organising the flowers for the wedding, the groom pays for the flowers for bride, bridesmaids, and flower girl, buttonholes for himself and the male attendants, both sets of parents and any special guests such as grandparents.

The buttonholes should be delivered to the ceremony by the florist or the best man, and they are worn pinned to the left lapel, stem pointing down. As a nice touch, the groom can wear a flower from the bride's bouquet. The best man's buttonhole should vary slightly — perhaps being a different shade — from those of the groomsmen and ushers.

GIFTS FOR ATTENDANTS

The stag party or rehearsal is a handy time to thank those who are helping to make your wedding day special. As well as handwritten thank-you notes, buy small gifts for the men in the bridal party, such as initialled key rings, pens, money clips, silver hip flasks or cuff links.

GROOM'S CHECKLIST

The following checklist will help you make sure everything gets done in good time:

SIX MONTHS BEFORE
- Start drawing up your guest list and ask your parents to do the same.
- Visit the clergy or registrar to discuss the ceremony.
- Decide, with your partner, how many ushers are needed (one for every fifty guests is a good guide).
- Ask a close friend or relative to be your best man, and select groomsmen and ushers.
- Discuss honeymoon plans, pick up brochures and consult a travel agent.
- If travelling abroad, update your passport, arrange for visas, international driver's licence (if necessary) and any vaccinations or innoculations you may need.
- Go with your partner, if you've decided to register for wedding gifts.

THREE MONTHS BEFORE
- Complete guest list, get final list from your parents and, with your partner, create a master list.
- Complete honeymoon plans and buy tickets.
- Order wedding rings.
- See your doctor and dentist for a check up.
- Resolve to eat, exercise and sleep well.
- Organise transport for the wedding day.

SIX TO EIGHT WEEKS BEFORE
- Decide on wedding clothes for yourself and your groomsmen and hire.
- Meet with best man to go over his responsibilities and those of the ushers.
- Shop for honeymoon clothes.
- Make arrangements for out-of-town guests.
- Buy a gift for your partner.
- Choose gifts for the best man and ushers to be given on the wedding day or at the stag party.
- Pick up wedding rings.

– Write thank-you notes.

TWO WEEKS BEFORE
– Arrange with best man for transport from the reception to overnight accommodation, and then to airport or train station.
– Double-check honeymoon reservations and necessary documentation.

ONE WEEK BEFORE
– Enjoy the stag party.
– Put the clergymember's or registrar's fee in a sealed envelope and give it to the best man to be delivered after the ceremony.
– Arrange traveller's cheques for the honeymoon.
– Make sure credit cards are valid for the duration of your honeymoon and check current credit limit. Pay outstanding balances, if necessary.
– Pack for the honeymoon.
– Arrange to move all belongings to your new home.
– Give gifts to male members of the wedding party.

WEDDING DAY
– Don't panic.
– Get to the church on time.
– Smile at the bride as she walks down the aisle.
– Relax and have a great day!

AFTER THE HONEYMOON
– Change all necessary documentation — legal, medical, financial — to reflect married status.
– Review both your insurance provisions, including life, property, car, medical and household, and change as necessary.

Go nine times to Lough Derg and you will find a husband, according to an old tradition.

GROOM'S AND GROOMSMEN'S PLANNER

Name		Tel.
Height	Weight	Cost £
Jacket	Trouser	
Shirt	Shoe Size	Top hat
Waistcoat	Bowtie	
Cummerbund	Cufflinks	Gloves

Name		Tel.
Height	Weight	Cost £
Jacket	Trouser	
Shirt	Shoe Size	Top hat
Waistcoat	Bowtie	
Cummerbund	Cufflinks	Gloves

Name		Tel.
Height	Weight	Cost £
Jacket	Trouser	
Shirt	Shoe Size	Top hat
Waistcoat	Bowtie	
Cummerbund	Cufflinks	Gloves

Company	Tel.
Address	
Contact	Style
Number ordered	Cost £

NOTES

TRANSPORT PLANNER

Number of cars needed _____ For _____
_____
_____
_____

Car hire company _____ Contact _____
Address _____ Tel. _____
Cost _____
Collect from _____ Take to _____
Car details (make, model, colour, decorations, chauffeur's dress)
_____
_____
_____
_____

Car hire company _____ Contact _____
Address _____ Tel. _____
Cost _____
Collect from _____ Take to _____
Car details (make, model, colour, decorations, chauffeur's dress)
_____
_____
_____
_____
_____

NOTES

9 THE SUPPORTING CAST

The number of attendants that make up your wedding party is largely dependent on the type of wedding you are planning. The larger and more formal the wedding, the greater the number of attendants. At the very least, a chief bridesmaid and best man is all that is required.

Often brides have two or three bridesmaids but the number can be as great as twelve, while the number of ushers usually depends on the size of the guest list. One usher is needed for every fifty guests. Don't worry if there are more ushers than bridesmaids: the numbers don't necessarily need to be the same.

THE CHIEF BRIDESMAID

The chief bridesmaid, also called the 'maid of honour' or 'matron of honour' if she is married, acts as an official witness along with the best man at your wedding. She is usually someone very close to you — a sister, cousin or best friend. Her duties, although not vitally important to the day, do require a certain amount of maturity. It is best to choose someone who can lend an ear or hand, when needed. Among the the tasks she may be called on to perform are addressing invitations, keeping track of wedding gifts, supervising the other bridesmaids and organising pre-wedding parties. Other duties include:

- Be a good friend.
- Offer to run errands, make phone calls to the florist, etc and see to other wedding details.
- Host or co-host the hen party.
- Help the bride get ready on the morning of the wedding.
- Keep a watchful eye over the other bridesmaids.
- Arrange the bride's veil and train before and during the

ceremony.
- Hold the bride's bouquet during the ceremony.
- Act as a witness to the ceremony and sign the register.
- Stand in the receiving line and mix with guests.
- Help the bride change into her going-away outfit.
- Make sure the bride's luggage and going-away outfit are taken to the reception for the honeymoon.
- Ensure the bride's passport is packed.
- Take care of the bride's gown and any accessories while the bride is on honeymoon.

THE BEST MAN

The best man is just what the name implies — the best man. And as such, he should be someone (a brother, uncle or close friend) who can help you to plan the wedding. The groom is not the only one to have a list of things to do before the wedding. After the couple themselves, the best man is the most important person involved in planning the day. In addition to the stag night and looking after the rings, his duties include:
- Co-ordinate with the bride and groom on all the information about the ceremony and reception.
- Organise the stag night, preferably a week before the wedding, and make sure things don't get out of hand.
- Help the groom to get ready.
- Make sure the groom gets to the church on time.
- Check that Order of Service booklets are ready for handing out.
- Take charge of the ushers, brief them on special seating arrangements and other responsibilities.
- Check that the groom, ushers and the fathers of the couple have their buttonholes.
- Look after the wedding ring until the proper moment during the ceremony.
- Act as official witness and sign the register.
- Escort the chief bridesmaid in the procession back down the aisle and out of the church.
- Pay any necessary fees on the day.
- Stand to the right of the groom during the ceremony.
- Ensure that the bridal party and all guests have transport to the

reception.

- See that all guests are enjoying themselves and have a drink of their choice.
- When the meal is about to begin, help usher guests into the dining area.
- After the meal, announce the cutting of the cake.
- Act as master of ceremonies at the reception.
- Begin speeches and reading of telegrams or messages.
- Check tickets, reservations, train connections, etc. for the honeymoon, and make sure the tickets are in the groom's pocket after he has changed clothes.
- Make sure the couple's luggage is at the hotel or in the car ready for a fast getaway.
- Help the couple get away.
- Take charge of the groom's wedding clothes and return the suit if rented.
- Deposit any cash gifts presented at the reception.
- Make sure all guests have a means of getting home.

BRIDESMAIDS

Bridesmaids are generally close friends or relatives of the bride and may be of any age, although very young girls are usually asked to be flower girls. If the groom has a sister you may wish to include her but it is not absolutely necessary. These days, bridesmaids should be prepared to pay their own expenses to and from the wedding and their own accommodation. Traditionally the bride's family pays for their outfits but with soaring wedding costs, it is not unusual for the bridesmaids to help pay for all or most of the expense. Among the bridesmaids' duties are:

- Be a good friend.
- Assist the bride whenever possible.
- Attend the rehearsal.
- Ensure other guests have a good time.

GROOMSMEN AND USHERS

Groomsmen and ushers, like bridesmaids, are generally close friends or relatives of the groom and sometimes, the bride. They don't have many duties to perform but the ones they oversee are important:

- Arrive at the venue for the ceremony at least forty-five minutes before the ceremony begins.
- Stand at the door and greet guests as they arrive.
- Ask each arriving guest if he or she is a friend of the bride or of the groom. Offer his right arm to the woman and escort her to the left side of the church if she is a friend of the bride; right side if a friend of the groom. If there are more guests seated on one side than the other, seating may be mixed.
- As the guests arrive, hand them an Order of Service booklet.
- Just before the bride arrives, escort the groom's mother to her seat and, just prior to the processional, escort the bride's mother.
- Bring umbrellas to the ceremony and reception to protect the bridal party and guests in case of bad weather.

FATHER OF THE BRIDE

The father of the bride has one of the most important and symbolic tasks — walking his daughter down the aisle to her groom. Other duties are:

- After walking his daughter down the aisle to the groom, takes his place on her left at the chancel steps (if a church ceremony), and if the celebrant asks 'Who giveth this woman ...', step forward and silently place his daughter's right hand in the celebrant's, step back to stand beside his wife in the front lefthand pew.
- If the wedding party adjourns to the vestry for the signing of the register, escort the groom's mother there and afterwards back down the aisle to her seat.
- At the reception greet guests with his wife, at the head of the receiving line.
- Make a speech and propose a toast at the reception to the health and future happiness of his daughter and her new husband.

FATHER OF THE GROOM

The father of the groom has few responsibilities at his son's wedding but he should:

- Escort the bride's mother to the vestry for the signing of the register and afterwards back down the aisle to her seat.
- At the reception stand next to his wife in the receiving line to

greet guests.
- If called on to speak at the reception, give a brief speech thanking the bride's parents for hosting the wedding and toast the health and happiness of his son and new daughter-in-law.

FLOWER GIRL

The flower girl can be a young relative (from three to eight years old) or the daughter of a close friend. Her duty is to carry a basket of flower petals to scatter down the aisle, or pass out single flowers to guests seated nearest the aisle as she walks up in the processional. If she is very young, she can take part in the procession and then take a seat near the front pew. At the end of the ceremony she and the ring bearer can follow the bride and groom in the recessional.

RING BEARER

The ring bearer is a young boy, usually less than eight but more than three, who walks up the aisle at the beginning of the ceremony with the wedding rings tied with ribbon to a satin pillow. If the actual ring(s) are being held by the best man, an inexpensive ring can be substituted. Like the flower girl, the ring bearer does not have to stand with the bridal party thoughout the entire ceremony and can follow the bride and groom in the recessional.

OUT-OF-TOWN GUESTS

Your wedding day may be the first time you have seen distant relatives and old friends in years. Make them feel extra special by preparing for their arrival and departure, and organising fun and interesting things for them to see and do in between. You will be surprised just how little you need to do to show them how much you appreciate their coming.

TRANSPORT

Find out when and where guests are arriving and make arrangements for a family member or close friend to meet them. If a guest wants to rent a car, send brochures about local car rental companies. The *Golden Pages* is a quick and easy way to gather information. Also include a detailed map and directions. This is easy to prepare and will be appreciated.

Do not leave guests stranded. Be sure they have transport back to the airport, ferry, or train station when the wedding is over. If you have a lot of out-of-town guests, simplify things by organising lifts for the first three days after the festivities. If guests wish to stay longer, they will gladly find their own transport.

ACCOMMODATION

When out-of-town friends make the effort to come to your wedding, you should ensure they have somewhere to stay. You might invite some guests to stay with you, at your parents home or with relatives or even close friends. Some guests may prefer to stay in a hotel or bed & breakfast, if so provide them with a list of local places and the prices. Be sure to take distances into consideration, try to keep guests centrally located and in close proximity to yourselves, other guests and the wedding ceremony.

ITINERARY

Have a wedding packet ready for each out-of-town guest, include maps, telephone numbers, invitations to any events relating to the wedding (such as the bridal shower or stag party), local information (shops, pubs, museums and interesting sights nearby). (If you prefer this could be included with the invitation, giving your guests a chance to plan their trip in advance.) If you want to go all out, include a local newspaper or a copy of a magazine like *In Dublin* or *Image*. Bord Fáilte has most of this information available free of charge at their branches around the country. Also be sure to include a note saying how happy you are that they have come so far for this special occasion.

It was while Tiernan O'Rourke, Prince of Breifne was praying at Lough Derg in the twelfth century that his wife Dervorgilla eloped with a neighbouring chieftain. In the ensuing war, the chieftain called on Strongbow for assistance, thus bringing the Normans to Ireland.

VISITING GUESTS' SCHEDULE

Guest _____ Tel. _____

Date/Time of arrival _____

Place of arrival _____

Being met by _____

Staying at _____ Tel. _____

Date/Time of departure _____

Place of departure _____

Transport _____

Guest _____ Tel. _____

Date/Time of arrival _____

Place of arrival _____

Being met by _____

Staying at _____ Tel. _____

Date/Time of departure _____

Place of departure _____

Transport _____

Guest _____ Tel. _____

Date/Time of arrival _____

Place of arrival _____

Being met by _____

Staying at _____ Tel. _____

Date/Time of departure _____

Place of departure _____

Transport _____

Guest _____ Tel. _____

Date/Time of arrival _____

Place of arrival _____

Being met by _____

Staying at _____ Tel. _____

Date/Time of departure _____

Place of departure _____

Transport _____

10   A GREAT RECEPTION

A really fun wedding reception is easy to organise if you take time early on to think about the possibilities, make your decisions and plan. The two of you should sit down together and talk about the type of reception you would like. Ask yourselves questions like how many guests you want to invite, and where and when you would like the reception to be held.

You will, of course, need to keep your budget in mind. It is easy to go overboard. A little careful planning now can save you from unnecessary spending later. If one or both of your parents are helping to pay for the wedding, they should be consulted too. If your ideas clash with theirs, try to find some areas which are less important to you and compromise. Serious disagreements between you and your parents can arise when sorting out the details. If this does happen, remind everyone that this is a celebration and try to persuade them to keep their tempers in check! Let the experts — the florist, dressmaker, celebrant, etc — know there is a conflict, they may be able to help you find a happy solution.

SETTING A STYLE

Style may be divided into four different categories: ultra-formal; formal; semi-formal; and informal. You may find your ideas fall somewhere in between two different styles. Don't worry, there are no absolute rules and you are free to pick and choose different aspects of each so long as the overall effect is tasteful. The following guidelines, however, may be helpful when you come to talk to your wedding experts such as florist, musicians and so on.

ULTRA-FORMAL
 – Two hundred or more guests.

- The reception is an elaborate sit-down meal; champagne is served throughout.
- Invitations are engraved or printed.

FORMAL
- Up to two hundred guests.
- Elegant sit-down or buffet sit-down reception, champagne served throughout.
- Invitations are engraved or printed.

SEMI-FORMAL
- One hundred to one hundred and fifty guests.
- Sit-down dinner or buffet.
- Printed invitations.

INFORMAL
- Up to one hundred guests.
- Buffet or simple hors d'oeuvres.
- Handwritten or pre-printed invitations.

THE PERSONAL TOUCH

Just like the ceremony, a wedding reception should reflect the personalities of the people involved — namely the two of you. Theme weddings or a personal touch are easy to develop and will make your reception really stand out. For instance, if your wedding falls near a holiday your reception could take on a seasonal charm.

On Valentine's Day: The bride could wear a gown that is a champagne or soft pink shade, the groom's waistcoat might be in romantic florals in reds and pinks, bridesmaids might dress in berry velvet, pink satin or floral cottons, while the groomsmen wear red bowties. Even the flowers for the wedding and reception can add to the romantic theme by using a red, white, and pink colour scheme. A heart-shaped wedding cake with delicate edible or live flowers, place cards with Victorian style handwriting, heart-shaped chocolates to be served after the meal, pink champagne to be served for the toasts and a band that plays plenty of slow, romantic songs — all will give a romantic touch to the occasion.

Christmas time: Bridesmaids might wear velvet gowns in white, red or green, while the bride could wear a gown made from crisp green, white and reds of Scottish tartans which look very

Christmassy. The groom's waistcoat or bowtie could be made from the same fabric as the bride's dress or in red or green. Before the ceremony and during the reception, play Christmas songs or have a group of children sing carols, decorate the reception venue with poinsettias, pine cones, and wreaths, use pine cones, silver bells, or other ornaments as table centrepieces and give guests inexpensive tree ornaments as presents.

Other creative touches can be defined by colour. Using a dominant colour theme throughout can be very effective, especially for an at-home reception. White complements most styles and can be used for flowers, table linens, napkins and candles.

Or reflect a facet of your lives in the festivities. If the two of you are involved in the theatre, go all out and enact a medieval banquet. If horseriding is a hobby, arrive at the ceremony and reception on horseback or by carriage and serve a horseshoe-shaped cake. Love country and western? Have barbecue food served buffet-style, use red and white checked table cloths, get a country and western band and hire a caller to teach your guests to dance the Cotton-Eyed Joe or Achy-Breaky Heart. Anything is possible with a little thought!

Another possibility is to include as many Irish customs and traditions as possible. (This is especially nice if some of your guests are from other countries.) Ireland has a great equine tradition, so start by incorporating this into your wedding. The groom and best man can arrive to the ceremony on horseback and later the bride and groom can leave for the reception in a horse-drawn carriage. Use traditional Irish music during the ceremony. Ask your clergy or registrar about saying the wedding service in Irish. At the reception, serve plenty of Guinness and the wonderful seafood we are known for such as salmon, plaice, oysters, prawns and scallops. And what better way to keep the festivities going all night than with a céilí band, set dancing and the impromptu singing of some Irish ballads.

SELECTING THE VENUE

You know where the ceremony will be held, and you have established basic guidelines for spending and style, now you can focus your attention on selecting a venue. Recently, the possibilities have gone beyond homes, halls and hotels. Restaurants, museums, art galleries, yachts, gardens and barns are all good alternatives.

Whatever you decide, try to make a decision as quickly as possible. Popular hotels are sometimes booked up to a year in advance, making it difficult for late planners. Other venues may be very busy during holidays or over the summer.

Don't book a site until you have visited it first, and try to time your visit with another wedding so that you can check out crowd capacity, the layout of tables, the set-up for the band or DJ, waiter service, parking space and decorations. If possible, sample the food.

Hotels are popular reception venues because most of the work is done by the hotel staff, leaving little work for you and your families. If you are planning a hotel reception, your first step is to find one that is not too far from the place where your ceremony is taking place. If your favourite venue is more than half an hour away, you should consider hiring a coach to transport your guests. The next step is to see the banqueting manager to discuss price, flowers, menu, drinks, parking, a complementary changing room, and anything else that might be included in a wedding reception 'package'. Check that they can cater for guests' special needs — such as vegetarian meals or access for disabled guests. If prices seem high, do not hesitate to ask for alternatives which will bring the cost down.

If space is not a problem, an at-home reception can be more personal and create a better atmosphere. A marquee is the perfect solution for increasing space and an ideal answer to the weather problem. Prices vary considerably according to the size, style and the type of furnishings required. Use the *Golden Pages* to help you source possible suppliers.

THE RECEIVING LINE

To have or not to have — it is another of those personal decisions. If time is tight, a receiving line gives the two of you the opportunity to talk to and thank each and every one of your guests personally, albeit briefly. If you are having a religious ceremony the line can be formed at or near the entrance to the building. If weather and time permit, greet guests just outside the door.

Alternatively, the receiving line can be formed at the entrance of your home, hall, banquet room or hotel. If pictures are going to be taken at the reception, postpone them until you have had a chance to greet your guests. Then your guests can have a drink while you relax and have your photographs taken.

The bride's mother should always be the first person to greet guests. Once she has said hello, she introduces the guest to the groom's mother. Next to them stand the bride and groom, the chief bridesmaid and other bridesmaids. The two fathers, if they are to be included, stand to the left of their wives. The best man and other groomsmen usually circulate among the guests: however, they too can be included in the receiving line.

GUEST BOOK TABLE

The guest book table is a small table or pedestal where the guest book sits and is usually set up near the entrance to the reception, either near the coatroom or at the end of the receiving line. The table is simply decorated with a white table linen and a simple flower arrangement. Guest books and pens can be purchased at some bridal shops or card shops. Alternatively, you can buy a decorative pen and blank book at a stationers.

SEATING PLANS

Seating arrangements for a wedding reception are relatively flexible, except at the bride's table where the newly weds are seated as the centre of attention. Generally, only the celebrant, bridal party and couple's parents are seated at the head table. However, if there is enough room, husbands and wives of the bridal party may also be seated there. The bride and groom always sit at the centre of the table, the bride to the left of the groom. To the groom's right is the bride's mother, the groom's father, the chief bridesmaid, the best man, the celebrant and then bridesmaids and groomsmen alternate. To the bride's left sits her father, the groom's mother and then bridesmaids and groomsmen alternate.

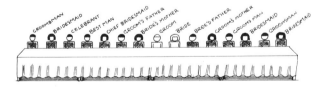

GUEST TABLES

Whether to plan seating for the rest of your guests is optional, but in general it does make things less confusing on the day. Seating arrangements should be well thought out so that guests have a clear view of the top table and the wedding cake. And mix and match your friends so that there will be good conversations.

Organise a 'singles' table for your unattached friends — you never know what might come of it. If there are small children, it is advisable to seat them with their parents. Seat relatives from both families together at some tables, they should enjoy sharing stories about the two of you. If there are several teenagers, they might prefer to have their own table too.

Organised table plans require a posted seating chart and place cards. Most hotel banqueting managers will provide you with both, but you may have to write the names yourself. The seating chart should be placed just outside the dining area. Place cards should be set at the table so guests can find their seats quickly.

SAYING GRACE

After guests have been seated or before they get in line for the buffet is the perfect time to say grace if you wish. If a clergy member is present, it is nice to ask him or her to say a few words of thanks for the day and meal. If not, one of you, your parents, or the best man may do so.

FOOD

The menu for your reception will be among the first things the hotel banqueting manager or caterer will want to discuss. Traditionally the wedding menu is a five-course meal: starter, soup, main course with a selection of seasonal vegetables, dessert, tea and coffee.

You should make arrangements for guests who may require special meals. Vegetarians and children, for example. Vegetarian dishes no longer consist of salads and crudites. Lovely meals can be organised at little extra cost. Ask the banqueting manager for suggestions. The simplest and most popular children's meal is chicken and chips. One other group who should not be forgotten are the people behind the scenes — the band, photographer, etc. Be sure to order a hearty sandwich or cold plate for them.

DRINK

What you serve to drink at the reception is up to you. Champagne is the traditional wedding drink, but couples can toast each other with wine, spirits, or something non-alcoholic. The drinks' bill can make up a large portion of your overall costs so make this decision carefully. In some parts of the country, sherry receptions are very popular — with the added bonus that sherry tends to be less expensive than other spirits.

If you want to serve something unique, a punch made with alcohol is refreshing and light. (Several recipes for fruit punches are included in Chapter 11.) A wine reception is always a good choice and there are many inexpensive but good wines available. Or, if the day is cold, your guests might appreciate a hot drink such as mulled wine, Irish coffee or hot port.

SPEECHES

Your best man will act as Master of Ceremonies for the evening. It is his duty to see that speeches and toasts are made at the right time and in the proper order. After the meal the best man announces the cutting of the cake. Champagne is served to guests, and the best man calls on the bride's father to make the first speech.

This speech should be brief but light and warm-hearted. The bride's father should welcome his new son-in-law into the family, thank the clergy, and say something nice about his new in-laws. Lastly, he proposes the first toast to the happy couple.

Next the best man stands to read some of the telegrams and cards that have been sent and then he calls on the groom to speak. The groom should toast his bride, thank his in-laws for giving them a wonderful wedding, thank his own parents for their love and support, thank the best man for his help, and conclude by toasting the bridesmaids.

As it is not customary for the bridesmaids to reply — though increasingly they do — the best man thanks the groom on their behalf, and then delivers his own speech. This should reflect the spirit of the day and should be funny, warm and sincere without being sentimental. Nor should it be too risqué — a good rule is to keep the bride and groom's parents in mind: if they could be upset by what is said, then don't say it. Finally, the best man asks everyone present to raise a glass and toast the newly wed couple.

It is becoming increasingly popular for the groom's father and the bride herself to say a few words. This is best organised in advance — few people can deliver a good speech off the cuff. If the groom's father or the bride is going to speak, the best man should be prepared to call on them at pre-designated times. The groom's father should speak after the bride's and the bride should speak after the groom.

THE FIRST DANCE

Afternoon and evening receptions usually involve dancing which means the two of you will be expected to lead with the first dance. Make arrangements in advance with the DJ or band leader. Decide which song you would like to dance to — a waltz is a favourite — and whether the best man or band leader will make the announcement.

When the announcement is made, you both walk out on to the dancefloor. Once you have shared the spotlight for a few minutes your parents, chief bridesmaid, best man, brothers and sisters and other wedding attendants may come on to the floor with their partners and join in. The bride's father may cut in and finish the dance with his daughter. If this happens, the groom should then ask the bride's mother to finish the dance. After the first dance, guests are welcome to join the bridal party.

TOSSING THE BOUQUET AND GARTER

Tossing the bouquet and garter is usually done just before you leave the reception. It can be done before you change into your going-away clothes or minutes before you make your grand exit. When talking through details with your band leader or DJ, be sure to make arrangements for when the toss will be announced.

When tossing the bouquet, the bride stands at the front of the dancefloor or on a chair with all the single, female guests behind her. She tosses the bouquet over her head and, or so the superstition goes, the woman who catches the flowers will be the next woman in the room to marry.

Tossing the garter is exactly like tossing the bouquet, but only the single, male guests participate. The groom removes the garter from his bride's leg — gently. If the bride is uncomfortable with this part of the tradition, she may hand the garter to the groom instead. He then tosses it over the heads of the men gathered before him. As with the bouquet, the man who catches the garter is thought to be the next man in the room to marry.

Some couples don't like the idea of giving away the flowers and garter, preferring to keep them as mementos. In this case, buy a second garter (which can be worn by the bride during the day) and a smaller bouquet and toss them instead.

DEPARTURE

When the bride and groom are ready to leave, they usually go to separate rooms to change into their going-away clothes. The best man accompanies the groom and the chief bridesmaid assists the bride. The couple rejoin the reception and spend a few moments thanking their parents. If there are any guests who have made a special effort to be at the wedding, they too should be thanked in person.

When you are ready to leave, the DJ or band leader makes an announcement and everyone moves towards the exit. Traditionally, guests throw rice, confetti or rose petals at the couple as they leave, a custom which symbolises luck and happiness. You should consult with the banqueting manager about any regulations they may have. You then run through the gathering of family and friends to a waiting car and drive away to your wedding night accommodation.

If you are staying at the hotel where the reception took place, you or your driver can take a scenic tour of the area or drive around for a few minutes. This gives guests time to move away from the entrance and allows the two of you to sneak back into the hotel a little later, through a different entrance.

A bride is known to have power over fairies unless she takes both feet off the floor in a dance. If she does this, then the fairies will regain the upper hand.

RECEPTION PLANNER

Keep track of reception venues, caterers, food, drink, equipment and other necessities on the following pages:

Estimate no. 1

Venue

Address

Manager   Tel.

Menu

Drinks

Cost £   Deposit £   Balance due £

Estimate no. 2

Venue

Address

Manager   Tel.

Menu

Drinks

Cost £   Deposit £   Balance due £

Estimate no. 3

Venue

Address

Manager   Tel.

Menu

Drinks

Cost £   Deposit £   Balance due £

Final Selection

Venue

Address

Manager   Tel.

Menu

Drinks

Cost £   Deposit £   Balance due £

Sundry

Equipment (rented chairs, tables, etc.)

Cost £   Deposit £   Balance due £

Services (waiters, bartenders, etc.)

Cost £   Deposit £   Balance due £

Miscellaneous (decorations, flowers, etc.)

Cost £   Deposit £   Balance due £

NOTES

11   RECEPTION AT HOME

An at-home reception can be the nicest, most intimate way of
sharing your wedding day with family and friends. And it can
also be the least expensive. Generally the reception takes place in the
bride's home which only adds to the feeling of joy. Your biggest
concern should be the amount of time and energy this type of
reception involves. The bigger the party, the more help you will
need. If friends and family offer to lend a hand, let them! Delegate
tasks like furniture arranging, food preparation, decorating, flower
arranging, etc. As the day draws nearer, you will really appreciate
their help and you'll also have great memories to share in the years
to come.

The secret of a great reception is preparation and planning. Start by
using the pages at the end of this chapter to outline what needs to be
done. Details to keep in mind are space, timing, parking facilities,
food, cake, drinks, crockery, staff (to serve food and drinks), music,
decorations and flowers. Once you see exactly what needs to be done
you will be better prepared to tackle each job at hand.

Space may be the biggest problem you have to overcome as the
average home only holds between fifty and sixty people
comfortably. If weather permits (which, in Ireland, it probably
won't!) you could increase your space by allowing guests access to
the garden. But, because the Irish weather is so unpredictable, it
might be best to hire a marquee. They come in a variety of sizes,
colours, and styles and the cost will vary so telephone several
companies to find the best rate. The vendor will ask you if you need
heaters, sockets, lights, tables, chairs, a floor, windows, doors,
stands, etc. If you are planning a formal sit-down meal, then the

answer is yes, you will need most of these items. However, if your reception is more informal, steer clear of ordering too many accessories (such as tables and chairs) as they increase your costs quickly and may get in the way of dancing and socialising. Two things you probably will need are extra sockets and a floor. If the weather is cold, you may also need a heater. These items, though fairly basic, can make all the difference to your guests' comfort.

Worrying about parking may seem like taking things too seriously, but it is important. The last thing you need is an angry neighbour complaining about a car blocking his or her house. Try to head off trouble by letting your neighbours know about the reception a week or two before the day. If you don't know them, write a brief note explaining the situation and drop it in their letterbox. Most people will be so pleased for you that they won't mind the inconvenience for one night.

Also, think about planning the layout of the party. Where will the band set up, the cake be cut, guests dance, food and drinks be served, etc? Go from room to room and imagine how the space can best be used. Does some furniture need to be moved in order to accommodate your plans? Make these decisions now, and save yourself unnecessary hassle later.

Do you have enough glasses, dishes, cutlery and linen to get you through the reception? Make a list of everything needed. If your reception is small enough you might be able to borrow most things from friends. If not, hire them from a caterer, marquee company or party hire company. Before placing an order, ask about the company's policy on delivery, collection, breakage and insurance. Have deliveries made the day before the reception. Just in case you forget, most of the items you may need are listed at the end of this chapter.

MENUS

Before planning the menu for the reception, decide whether to prepare the food yourself or hire a caterer. Making the food yourself may save you money, but will add a great deal to your workload. If friends and family are willing to help, assign them dishes, but let them know you need at least three days' warning if they change their minds. Though expensive, hiring a caterer frees you from the worry of having to prepare and present the food — and of having to organise others.

When you plan your menu, take into consideration the time of day and the season. On a chilly afternoon, guests will prefer a steaming cup of coffee and hot quiche to cold drinks and sandwiches. If the wedding is in the early afternoon and the reception follows immediately, a light buffet (a variety of sweet and savoury dishes) and sherry reception would be ideal. After a small morning wedding, serve brunch and Bloody Marys. If you're having a traditional wedding, however, you will probably want a traditional wedding breakfast (formal luncheon). Typically this would include red and white wine, starter, soup and a roll or brown bread, main course, dessert, petits fours and coffee or tea. When the wedding cake is cut, a glass of champagne or sparkling wine is served to drink to the toasts. Sample menus might include:

Fresh salmon salad	Melon and port wine
Consommé	Vegetable soup
Prime rib	Chicken supreme
with a selection of vegetables	with a selection of vegetables
Profiteroles	Apple tart and vanilla ice cream
Coffee or tea	Coffee or tea

The following suggestions may be used in a sit-down meal, buffet or cocktail reception:

Hors d'oeuvres	Chicken salad	Quiche
Meatballs	Chilled fruit salad	Kebabs
Cocktail sausages	Terrine smoked salmon	
Stuffed filo triangles		**Accompaniment**
Salmon on soda bread	**Soups**	Coleslaw
Chicken vol au vent	Minestrone soup	Rice salad
Sandwiches	Tomato soup	Potato salad
Crudites	Carrot soup	Vegetables in season
Dips	Vegetable soup	
Crackers	Mushroom soup	**Desserts**
Nuts	Leek and potato soup	Fruit salad
Pretzels		Ice cream
Crisps	**Main Courses**	Cheesecake
Starters	Cold or hot fillet of beef	Profiteroles
Pate	Cold or hot baked ham	Fruit tarts
Salmon mousse	Sliced turkey	Strawberries and cream
Egg mayonnaise	Prawns	Chocolate dipped
Green salad	Chicken drumsticks	strawberries
Tomato and onion salad	Lasagne	Chocolate souffle

If you are preparing the food yourself you need to have an idea of approximate quantities. The following is an estimate of the amounts needed for a reception with fifty guests.

Hors d'oeuvres : If you are serving hors d'oeuvres before a meal, limit the serving time to one-and-a-half hours — you don't want guests to fill up too soon. Plan for a mix of four different hors d'oeuvres and about three hundred individual pieces.

Soups and Starters: Unless you are planning a sit-down meal, soup should be replaced by a more easily handled starter like paté or salmon. Allow for about 5lb of each, if serving both, and four to six large loaves of bread or seventy rolls.

Meats: Chicken, turkey, lamb, beef and pork are popular with most guests. Prepare 16lb of boneless chicken or turkey, or between 16-20lb of lamb, beef or pork.

Vegetables: Most hotels serve two vegetables and a potato dish. You will need 16lb of potatoes and 12lb of vegetables.

Cheese: 4-5lb should be more than enough after dinner. If serving before, plan for 10-12lb and serve cubed for convenience. Try cheddar, brie, camembert, herb, smoked, blue, gouda and Jarlsberg cheese. You will also need plenty of bread or crackers. Mix flavours and include plain, wheat, rye and sesame breads.

Coffee: If you are serving drinks at the reception, it is always a good idea to serve coffee — 3lb of ground coffee, one litre of cream, and one half pound of sugar should be plenty.

DRINKS

Traditionally, the first drink offered at an Irish reception is sherry. Nowadays, few young people like sherry, but it is often served as a courtesy to older guests. Red or white wine is usually available with the meal. Champagne is, of course, the traditional drink for toasting the couple's health and happiness. Frequently, sparkling wine is substituted as a less expensive option. Today, many sparkling wines are made in the fashion of champagne and few people can taste the difference.

In addition to alcohol, non-alcoholic drinks should be made available. Soft drinks, sparkling and still mineral water, tea, coffee and juice are the obvious choices. If you would like something new, try one of the following fruit drinks:

LADY PRIMROSE PUNCH (Serves 25)

½ pint water	½ pint granulated sugar

450ml pineapple and strawberry syrup (Use canned fruit in syrup.
Reserve fruit to put into punch when serving.)

450ml fresh orange juice	225ml strong tea
450ml grape juice	200ml maraschino cherries
4 pints cold water	

2 pints sparkling white lemonade or ginger ale (champagne or
sparkling wine can be substituted to make a champagne punch)

Boil ½ pint water and the sugar for ten minutes stirring constantly.
Remove from heat. Set aside ¼ pint. To the remainder add the other
ingredients, and stir. Add cold water and lemonade just before serving.

SPICY CRANBERRY PUNCH (Serves 15-20)

½ pint water	125g sugar
4 cinnamon sticks	12 whole cloves
1 pint cranberry juice	¾ pint fresh orange juice
¾ pint pineapple juice	4 pints tonic (or champagne)

Combine water, sugar, cinnamon and cloves in saucepan. Boil, stirring
constantly, until sugar dissolves. Reduce heat. Add cranberry juice and
cook over low heat for five minutes. Allow to cool. Remove spices and
add pineapple and orange juice. Just before serving add tonic water.

Whatever drinks you choose, buy them from your wine merchant on
a sale or return basis. This means you can return any unopened
containers or bottles. Many shops will also supply glasses for the day
at no extra charge. Plan on at least half a bottle of wine per guest and
six glasses of champagne or sparkling wine to a bottle.

HIRING HELP

If you are going to the trouble of organising your wedding reception,
allow yourselves one luxury — hired help. You usually need about
one waiter for every fifteen guests and one bartender.

Help can be provided by a party hire company or catering firm,
but the least expensive help is probably available from the local pub.
The day before the reception, ask the people involved over for a

briefing. Explain where everything will be, and leave specific instructions for serving and refilling glasses. Also, appoint a friend or relative as supervisor so you can relax and enjoy the celebration.

WEDDING CAKE

The focal point of the reception will be your wedding cake. Guests will gather round it, and your photographer will want to take at least one picture of the two of you standing by it. Traditionally, the Irish wedding cake is a rich fruit cake covered in almond paste and white royal icing. The cake itself is not too difficult to make although the icing may be best left to the professionals. Your mother or a friend might have a secret recipe, so be sure to ask. If not, bakeries and cake makers are easy to find in the *Golden Pages* under 'Bakers and Confectioners'. If someone is willing to bake your wedding cake, get them to do so as early as possible: these cakes really improve with age. And if you would like to add a little zing, pour some whiskey or brandy over the cake just after removing it from the oven. The following is a delicious traditional wedding cake recipe from the kitchen of Mrs Bee Mannix-Walsh of the Cookery Centre of Ireland:

Lower tier:	*Middle tier:*	*Top tier:*
15 oz raisins	9 oz raisins	3 oz raisins
15 oz sultanas	9 oz sultanas	3 oz sultanas
20 oz currants	12 oz currants	4 oz currants
10 oz mixed peel	6 oz mixed peel	2 oz mixed peel
5 oz prunes	3 oz prunes	1 oz prunes
5 oz dates	3 oz dates	1 oz dates
5 oz cherries	3 oz cherries	1 oz cherries
1 apple	½ apple	½ apple
3 oz chopped almonds	3 oz chopped almonds	1 oz chopped almonds
3 oz ground almonds	3 oz ground almonds	1 oz ground almonds
½ tsp grated nutmeg	¼ tsp nutmeg	¼ tsp nutmeg
½ tsp mixed spice	¼ tsp mixed spice	¼ tsp mixed spice
Grated rind of 1 lemon	Grated rind of ½ lemon	Grated rind of ¼ lemon
15 oz butter	9 oz butter	3 oz butter
15 oz sugar (Barbados)	9 oz sugar	3 oz sugar
10 eggs	6 eggs	2 eggs
19 oz flour	11 oz flour	4 oz flour
Cover with	*Cover with*	*Cover with*
Almond paste 1½ lb	Almond paste 1lb	Almond paste 6 oz
Water icing ¾lb	Water icing ½ lb	Water icing 4 oz
Royal icing 2½lb	Royal icing 2lb	Royal icing ¾ lb

1. Prepare fruit and mix it with spice, nuts and lemon rind.
2. Cream butter and sugar.
3. Break in an egg and beat until mixture thickens, mix in a little sieved flour. Continue in this way until all eggs have been added.
4. Add remainder of flour.
5. Stir in prepared fruit and mix thoroughly.
6. Put into prepared tin and bake in very moderate oven.

SIZE OF TIN AND BAKING TIME

Lowest tier	Middle tier	Top tier
12-inch tin	9-inch tin	6-inch tin
About 6 hours	About 3½ hours	About 1¾ hours

ALMOND PASTE

1 lb ground almonds	1 tbs whiskey	1 lb castor sugar
1 tbs sherry	¼ tsp almond essence	2 eggs
¼ tsp ratafia essence	1 dsp orange flower water	

1. Crush lumps out of almonds and sieve castor sugar, mix both well together.
2. Beat eggs, add flavouring, sherry and whiskey. Keep a little of the egg white back for brushing over cake.
3. Pour slowly into almonds and sugar and mix to stiff paste.
4. Turn onto sugared board and knead well. Roll out and use as required.

WATER ICING

½ lb icing sugar   Boiling water
Flavouring and colouring as desired

1. Sieve icing sugar and put into bowl.
2. Add boiling water slowly until it is the consistency of thick cream.
3. Add flavouring and colouring and beat until smooth and glossy.

ROYAL ICING

1 lb icing sugar	2 whites of eggs	1 teasp glycerine
Juice of 1 lemon	A few drops of laundry blue	

1. Roll out sugar on kitchen paper. Put through wire sieve and then through hair sieve.
2. Mix with half beaten white of egg, lemon juice and glycerine.
3. Beat for fifteen minutes.

Should you decide to let a professional bake the cake, visit a few bakeries first and ask to sample a slice. This is a standard request and most are willing to comply. Also ask to see their portfolio (usually a photo album featuring pictures of cakes the baker has made). You will be delighted to know that cakes come in a variety of shapes, sizes and colours. It is not unusual these days to see a heart, clover or horseshoe-shaped cake.

For couples wanting something just a bit different there are quite a few options. Pavlova wedding cakes are available and make a lovely and light alternative. Sponge cake, the traditional American wedding cake, is a possibility and comes in a variety of flavours including vanilla, spice and lemon. Or what could be lovelier than a pyramid of profiteroles bound together with spun sugar? For those who love chocolate, why not have a decadent chocolate cake? It is your wedding after all!

When it is time to cut the cake you need to have the proper utensils ready — a sharp knife, damp cloth and cake server. Traditional Irish wedding cakes can be very difficult to slice so you will want to have an incision already made. When you are done and the photographer has finished, either roll the cake into the kitchen to be served, or slice the pieces yourselves. The decision is yours but the latter is obviously more difficult, not to mention messy. Be sure to remove the top layer and set it aside for safe keeping. The Irish custom says it should be kept until the christening of your first baby, although you may wish to have some when celebrating your first anniversary. Wrapped carefully, a good quality fruit cake will last for several years. Another custom is to send a slice to those unable to attend the wedding.

FINISHING TOUCHES

Mints and nuts add a finishing touch to any reception. You can place them in small bowls around the house where guests will mingle, or wrap them in a small lace pouch tied with satin ribbon and leave them at the tables or near the coffee. At some Italian weddings sugar-coated almonds are left at guests' places. A tasty recipe for sugar-coated almonds and spiced nuts follows:

SUGARED ALMONDS

1 pint sugar	¼ pint water	1 tsp cinnamon
1 lb unblanched almonds		

Cook sugar, cinnamon and water in saucepan over slow heat, stirring constantly, then bring to rapid boil. When mixture is clear and drops heavily from spoon, add the almonds. Stir nuts until well coated. Remove from heat and stir on marble slab until dry. Sift to remove excess sugar.

SPICED NUTS

2 oz butter	½ tsp Tabasco Sauce	1 pint mixed nuts
2 tsp Worcestershire Sauce	1 tbs garlic salt	

Melt the butter in a saucepan, add spices and blend. Add nuts and coat well. Spread mixture on baking sheet and bake in a moderate oven for 20 minutes (or until lightly brown). Cool on a paper napkin.

DECORATIONS

Decorations, table settings and flowers are background props which help create a mood so they should tone in with the overall style of your wedding day. They can range from elaborate to simple, depending on your taste and budget.

To start, look at each room of your house as a blank canvas waiting to be designed. A cluttered mantlepiece, wiped clean, looks beautiful when covered with candlesticks of various shapes and sizes. A small sidetable, when decked with a pretty tablecloth and picture frames filled with family photos becomes a focal point for conversation. Balloons tied to the front gate or door let guests know they have arrived to a real celebration. Flowers, particularly one or two large arrangements, are elegant or romantic. Let your imagination run wild. Be creative. Try to give old standbys a new life. Christmas decorations for example, when gathered together in a crystal bowl, make for a beautiful centrepiece.

If your rooms are particularly bare, look into hiring plants and small trees from a florist or garden centre. Arrange several in a corner behind a love seat or group of chairs to create a nice backdrop for photographs. December receptions can make use of Christmas trees not only for decoration but as token presents for your guests. Tie handmade dough ornaments with satin ribbons to the tree for giving to your guests. Put your names and wedding date or a simple message of goodwill on them.

DOUGH ORNAMENTS

2 pints flour	½ pint salt	¾ pint water

Mix flour and salt in a large bowl, gradually adding water till mixture is firm but not sticky. Knead for three or four minutes. If dough is too soft, knead in more flour. Roll dough out on lightly floured grease paper. Make your own shapes or use pastry cutters. Using an old pencil, pierce a hole in the dough for threading later. Gently transfer to baking sheet, and bake for one hour at 150° or until ornaments are light brown. Remove from oven and let cool.

Personalise with paints or water colours, and bake again for fifteen minutes. Coat with polyurethane or clear nail varnish for keeping.

Or why not try crackers? Though usually seen only at Christmas there is no reason why you can't make them at any time of year.

WEDDING CRACKERS

For each cracker you need: coloured paper, thin white card, small gifts or candy, confetti, snaps (available from hobby shops), coloured string, scissors, double-sided tape, pencil, ruler, ribbon.

Cut three 10 x 18 cm rectangles of thin white card and place them on the reverse side of the 45 x 18 cm sheet of coloured paper 4 cm apart. Tape in place. Next put your confetti, small gift and snap in the centre of the paper and roll the card and coloured paper around them to form a tube. Tie cord around each end of the tube, being careful not to tear the paper, and fold the thin white card on each end to the inside. Decorate the cracker to match the colours of your wedding or the season. Use ribbon, stiff paper shapes, paint, markers, dried flowers, or just about anything you can think of using.

FLOWERS

Flowers, from the florist or your garden, add a special touch to any event. Colours and placement are two key things to keep in mind. The colours of your floral arrangements should echo those used in the wedding and those worn by the bridal party. Where possible, let flowers for the ceremony do double duty for the reception. Positioning is important when you want to create an impact. The more powerful a display, the fewer you will need and the more money you will save. An ideal place is near the entrance or in the room where the two of you will receive your guests or at the base of a staircase or in front of a fireplace. A garland looks lovely around columns outside or on the railing of a set of stairs. And don't forget the marquee. Wrap garlands of greenery around the main poles, and for an extra flourish of colour, use hanging baskets.

TABLE SETTINGS

Table settings are always a problem. The best advice is to choose a simple style and use sparkling clean linen, glassware, cutlery and plates.

A buffet is ideal when you are entertaining a large group. The table or counter you use should be set up to allow guests freedom to move and easy access to the food. The more cumbersome foods, such as meat, should be at the front of the table. Arrange other foods on the table attractively by mixing the height and size of serving bowls. Cutlery and napkins can be set on the table in neat rows or in baskets lined with linen napkins. If the buffet table gets crowded, use a second table for water and other drinks. Tall candles add to the elegance of the buffet table. Any other decorations should be kept to a minimum as they detract from the food and can get in the way of guests serving themselves.

A formal place setting is made up of dinner plate (if patterned, it should face the guest), butter plate (to the left of the fish fork), butter knife (across the butter plate), salad fork (left of the dinner plate), entrée fork (left of the salad fork), fish fork (left of the entrée fork), salad knife (to the right of the dinner plate), meat knife (right of the salad knife), fish knife, soup/fruit spoon (right of the salad knife), and napkin (in the centre of the dinner plate).

The things to remember are: the table is set from the outside in, so the cutlery for the first course is on the outside; knife blades should be placed with the cutting edge towards the plate; dessert spoons or forks are brought in on the dessert plate prior to serving dessert; and no more than three of any one piece of cutlery should be on the table (unless you serve oysters in which case you will need an oyster fork which is placed to the right of the soup spoon).

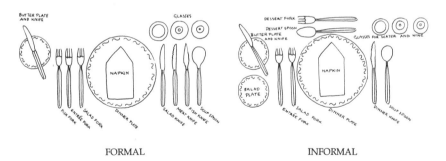

FORMAL   INFORMAL

An informal place setting includes dinner plate at the centre, salad fork to the left of the plate, entrée fork to its left, salad plate (left of the forks), butter knife across the butter plate, dinner knife (right of the dinner plate), soup spoon (right of the knife), dessert fork or spoon (above the dinner plate), and napkin in the centre of the dinner plate.

LINEN NAPKINS

Pretty folded napkins add a special touch to any formal table setting and they don't have to be difficult to make. Start by folding your napkin in half, and then fold it in half again. Turn it so a pointed corner faces you. Now fold the top corner (farthest from you) underneath so the top is flat. Fold the left and right sides underneath as well.

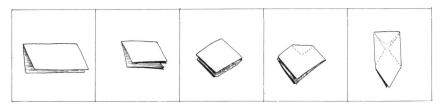

> *Eyes beaming with welcome shall throng round to light thee*
> *And Love serve the feast with his own willing hand*
>
>   *'Tho' humble the banquet' by Thomas Moore from* Irish melodies

RECEPTION EQUIPMENT ORGANISER

Serving Equipment/trays

Chafing dishes (to keep things hot)

Decorative baskets	Coffee urn
Teapot	Sugar bowl
Trays	Heated trolley

Serving dishes and bowls (in various sizes)

Jugs	Toothpicks
Doilies	Tablecloths and napkins

Bar Equipment

Corkscrews	Ice buckets
Bottle openers	Drink stirrers

Glassware

Wine glasses	
Beer glasses	Champagne glasses
Sherry glasses	Water tumblers

Cutlery

Knives	
Forks	Spoons
Serving spoons	Sharp knives

Dishware

Dinner plates	
Cake plates	Salad bowls
Side plates	Cups and saucers

Miscellaneous

Ashtrays	Toilet paper
Coat hangers	Candles
Hand towels	Ice cubes
Matches	Paper frills
Paper napkins	Salt and pepper shakers

RECEPTION ORGANISER

Food
_____
_____
_____
_____

Beverages
_____
_____
_____
_____
_____

Flowers
_____
_____
_____
_____
_____

Decorations
_____
_____
_____

Equipment (rented chairs, tables, etc.)
_____
_____
_____
_____

Cost £   Deposit £   Balance due £

Services (waiters, bartenders, etc.)
_____
_____
_____

Cost £   Deposit £   Balance due £

NOTES

12   INVITATIONS

An invitation to a wedding is not just an invitation to a big party. Rather, it is the first formal announcement to family and friends that your marriage is taking place, a request to others to join in the festivities. It is the indication to your guests of the style of your wedding.

Because an invitation conveys so much, careful thought should go into deciding who should receive one and how it should be delivered. But before these decisions can be made you will need to set a wedding date and time, meet with your clergy or visit the registry office, and book the ceremony and reception venues. Assuming all of this has been done, let's begin preparing the guest list.

DRAWING UP THE GUEST LIST

The easiest way to compile a guest list is for both of you and your parents to write down the names and addresses of everyone you would like to invite. Presumably this will include relatives, close friends, neighbours, your bridal party and their spouses or partners, the clergy (and his or her spouse, if appropriate), business friends, and friends from sports, church or social groups. Once you have all these names together, they become your master list.

Traditionally, the master list is divided equally between the bride and groom and their families. You probably have some joint friends as well. In some cases, one partner has a larger number of guests to invite than the other — that's perfectly acceptable. The only time this might present a problem is when it is the groom's list (or his parents') which is larger and the bride's parents are paying for the wedding. If this happens there are two possible solutions: either the list can be pared down to include close family and friends only, or the groom (and his family) can pay a share of the related costs.

Ideally, everyone on the master list can be invited, but more often than not some names will have to be dropped. If you are having difficulty deciding which names to drop, try dividing the master list in two and labelling one A and the other B. On the A list are those who absolutely must be invited. Invitations to these guests are sent six to eight weeks prior to the wedding. If some people from this list cannot attend, an invitation may then be sent to a person on the B list. Continue working your way down the B list in this way until three weeks before the wedding. (After this it is impolite to send invitations.)

Another potential problem can arise when you want to invite one or two people from a group, such as business colleagues, neighbours and distant relatives. If your guest list is limited it is always better not to invite anyone from the group, than to invite some people and not others. If you are really struggling with the decision of whether to invite or not, simply send an invitation to the evening celebration which takes place after the meal.

Once you have a final count, add a few extra for mistakes and as mementos for yourselves and your parents. An extra ten invitations for every hundred on the guest list is a realistic ratio.

DEALING WITH THE PRINTER

Wedding stationery is big business — it involves more than just invitations. There are Order of Service or Mass booklets, cake boxes, seals, napkins and a multitude of other wonderful items to consider. And just to make things a little more interesting, everything comes in a variety of papers, colours, sizes and styles. But before you get caught up in ordering everything, keep in mind that stationery costs mount up very quickly. It's not absolutely necessary to buy or order anything other than invitations.

Order your stationery at least three months before the wedding day to allow enough time for printing and postage. Invitations should be sent four to six weeks before your wedding day. When placing the order, you will need to know what stationery items you want and all your wedding details. The following outlines most of what is available:

Ceremony invitations: Designed for two purposes: to outline details of the wedding only; or to outline details of the wedding and reception.

Only one invitation is needed per family unless there are children over eighteen living in the household, in which case send each an individual invitation. Strictly speaking, members of your own families and the bridal party should be sent an invitation. If you feel uncomfortable about sending invitations to close family or friends, deliver them in person.

The wording for ceremony invitations should reflect the style you have chosen for the entire wedding and should set the tone for all other stationery.

Reception card: A separate invitation, slightly smaller than the wedding invitation, but similar in style, paper, colour and printing. It is used when details of the reception are not included on the ceremony invitation as, for instance, occurs when the church or registry office is too small or the ceremony invitations are ultra formal.

Evening invitation: Often when the ceremony is going to be a small and intimate affair, or if it is held at a registry office, only immediate family and close friends are invited to the reception and meal immediately following. Evening invitations to other guests refer to the celebration after the smaller group have had their meal.

Reply cards: Tucked inside the wedding invitation and extremely useful in today's busy world. This card is printed on the same paper and in the same style as the invitation. The wording is basic — guests can respond with an acceptance or regret and fill in the number of guests attending. A pre-printed envelope should be supplied for quick and easy return.

Order of Service or Mass booklet: Outlines the order of events of the wedding ceremony. It contains the names of the bridal party, any special dedication, name of the church, date and time of the ceremony, music selections, the processional, the officiant's or clergy's address, prayers and their responses, readings, hymns, the marriage service, signing the register and the recessional. Go over the information in detail with your officiant or clergy before having these booklets printed.

Place cards: Indicate where each guest sits at the reception meal.

Serviettes: Can be ordered with your names and the date of the wedding.

Matchboxes: Make nice keepsakes for guests and can be ordered with your names and wedding date on the cover.

Cake boxes: For sending cake to relatives and friends who cannot attend the reception.

Envelope seals: These are decorative stickers which can be used to seal the invitation envelope.

Note cards: Make ideal thank-you cards, change of address notices and general stationery after the wedding. They are usually printed on the same paper and in the same style as the wedding invitation.

Thank-you cards: Usually in a style that complements the wedding invitations. Should never be sent in lieu of a handwritten note but can be used when writing a thank-you note is not possible immediately.

The best way to avoid costly mistakes is to give the printer a typed or neatly handwritten page of your wedding details such as the time of the ceremony, the name and address of the venue, the time and location of the reception, and the names of the bridal party. Request a proof to check before the invitations are printed. Read it over carefully, looking for spelling or punctuation mistakes. Ask a friend to go over it as well. Correcting mistakes later can be very expensive — and annoying.

INVITATIONS

There are no rules. You are free to telephone guests or send formally engraved invitations, whichever you prefer. However, invitations set the tone and style for a wedding so be sure that whatever you decide is in keeping with your overall plan.

The *crème de la crème* of wedding invitations is white or ecru paper with black or silver engraving. (Engraving is a process which etches lettering deep into paper, and requires special printing plates and a coloured dye for the lettering.) These are the most formal invitations you can order, although not necessarily the most expensive.

If your budget does not stretch to such extravagance, consider thermography, another kind of printing which simulates engraving but doesn't require specially designed printing plates. It is a beautiful — and cost-saving — alternative.

Another money saving idea is pre-printed invitations. Usually these can be purchased in quantities of ten and come with matching evening invitations, thank-you notes and cake boxes. Prices range from £2.20 to £4 per pack. Check with local card or stationery shops for their product range.

If this seems too impersonal, why not try making invitations yourself? There are many lovely papers available that would make beautiful invitations. Look for handmade, marbled or recycled paper and then give your imagination free rein. Art, hobby and fabric shops are full of materials which could be used.

If you are having a small informal wedding, you may decide against written invitations altogether and telephone your guests personally. However, if you're planning a formal or semi-formal wedding, a written invitation is a must.

STYLES

There are a wide variety of invitation styles ranging from ultra-formal to informal. Formal invitations are printed on heavy white or ecru folded paper in black or silver ink. Generally, there is little if any decoration, with the exception of raised lettering and a thin rule around the edge. Often Roman or Script typefaces are used, both of which are easy to read.

Ultra-formal and formal invitations are written in the third person, request the 'honour' of a guest's presence rather than the 'pleasure', and may or may not have a line for writing in the guest's name. If all of your guests are invited to the reception, the place and time will appear on a separate reception card.

Formal and semi-formal invitations are similar to the ultra-formal except that they request the 'pleasure' rather than the 'honour' of a guest's presence. The card may be in soft peach, ivory or champagne and some feature flowers, bells, seashells or religious designs and a space is usually provided for filling in the guest's name by hand.

Informal invitations give a couple the widest scope for imagination as they can be telephoned, handwritten, printed or pre-printed. Your printer's sample books should contain a wide range of colours and designs so ask to browse through them. If you decide to handwrite or make your invitations, consider hiring a calligrapher to write and address them. Names and addresses can be found in the *Golden Pages* under 'Calligraphy'.

WORDING YOUR INVITATIONS

An ultra-formal invitation is usually issued by the bride's parents, and the wording is fairly straightforward. The printing is always centred on the page and capitalisation and punctuation are as follows:

Mr and Mrs David Murphy
request the honour of your presence
at the marriage of their daughter
Kathleen Marie
with
Mr John Paul Kelly
Saturday, the twenty-eighth of July
Nineteen hundred and ninety-six
at two o'clock
St Andrew's Church
Ennis, County Clare

As a separate reception card and reply card are included with ultra-formal invitations, there is no need to mention the celebration afterwards or give an RSVP.

An etiquette debate has been ongoing for several years now as to whether the phrase 'Black Tie' or 'Formal Attire' is acceptable on an invitation. If your wedding is to be an ultra-formal or formal affair, it is more correct to spread the dress code by word of mouth through family and friends rather than boldly printing it on the invitation. (For this reason it is left off the samples appearing here.)

Formal and semi-formal weddings give couples greater flexibility in wording the invitation. You might, if you prefer, send a separate reception and reply card. If so, omit the reception, RSVP and address information on the ceremony invitation. (This applies to the following examples.)

When the bride's parents are issuing the invitation, this format is most frequently used:

Mr and Mrs David Murphy
request the pleasure of the company of

_____

on the occasion of
the marriage of their daughter
Kathleen Marie
with

Mr John Paul Kelly
at St Andrew's Church
Ennis, Co Clare
on Saturday, 28th July, 1996
at 2.30 p.m.
and afterwards at a reception in
Green's Hotel
Ennis

6 Brookfield
Ennis, County Clare   RSVP

If the reception is being held in the home of the bride's parents, the above invitation would read:

Mr and Mrs David Murphy
request the pleasure of the company of

_____

on the occasion of
the marriage of their daughter
Kathleen Marie
with
Mr John Paul Kelly
at St Andrew's Church
Ennis, County Clare
on Saturday, 28th July, 1996
at 2.30 p.m.
and afterwards at home

6 Brookfield
Ennis, County Clare   RSVP

If the groom's parents are helping to pay for the wedding, their name can be added to the headline of the invitation if they wish:

Mr and Mrs David Murphy
and
Mr and Mrs James Kelly
request the pleasure of the company of

_____

on the occasion of
the marriage of their children
Kathleen Marie
and
Mr John Paul Kelly
at St Andrew's Church
Ennis, Co Clare

on Saturday, 28th July, 1996
at 2.30 p.m.
and afterwards at a reception in
Green's Hotel
Ennis

6 Brookfield
Ennis, County Clare   RSVP

If the two of you are hosting your own wedding but the overall style is formal or semi-formal, you may prefer the following:

Kathleen Marie Murphy
and John Paul Kelly
request the pleasure of the company of

_____

on the occasion of
their marriage
at St Andrew's Church
Ennis
on Saturday, 28th July, 1996
at 2.30 p.m.
and afterwards at a reception in
Green's Hotel
Ennis

6 Brookfield
Ennis, County Clare   RSVP

Informal invitations allow you to be most creative. They may be engraved, pre-printed or handwritten. Reception details and RSVP are written or printed on the card. Feel free to mix and match different parts of the following suggestions.

When the bride's parents issue an informal invitation it may read:

Dear _____
We would be pleased if you could attend
the marriage of our daughter
Kathleen Marie
with
John Kelly
at St Andrew's Church
Ennis
on Saturday, 28th July, 1996
at 2.30 p.m.
and afterwards at a reception in

Green's Hotel
Ennis

Mr & Mrs David Murphy
6 Brookfield
Ennis, County Clare   RSVP

Informal invitations or those being extended by both of you might read:

Kathleen Marie Murphy
and
John Paul Kelly
request the pleasure of the company of

_____

on the occasion of their marriage
at St Andrew's Church
Ennis
on Saturday, 28th July, 1996
at 2.30 p.m.
and afterwards at a reception in
Green's Hotel
Ennis

6 Brookfield
Ennis, County Clare   RSVP

or

Kathleen Murphy
and
John Kelly

Our joy would be more complete
if you would join us
in our celebration
of new beginnings at
St Andrew's Church
Ennis, County Clare
July 28, 1996 at 2.30 p.m.

Reception following at
Green's Hotel, Ennis, County Clare
6 Brookfield
Ennis, County Clare   RSVP

WORDINGS FOR SPECIAL CIRCUMSTANCES

Not every wedding is the same, so if you are looking for the wordings to special circumstances read through the following. Keep in mind though, that these and those above (except in the case of the ultra-formal) are guides only. If they do not appeal to you, develop your own wording along the same lines.

Double weddings:
Mr and Mrs David Murphy request the honour of your presence at the marriage of their daughters Kathleen Marie to Mr John Paul Kelly and Teresa to Mr Martin Fahey ...

The elder sister is mentioned first on the invitation.

When the bride's mother is widowed:
Mrs David Murphy requests the honour of your presence at the marriage of her daughter ...

When the bride's father hosts the wedding:
Mr David Murphy requests the honour of your presence at the marriage of his daughter ...

When the bride's mother and step-father host the wedding:
Mr and Mrs John Carr request the honour of your presence at the marriage of her daughter ...

When the bride's father and step-mother host the wedding:
Mr and Mrs David Murphy request the honour of your presence at the marriage of his daughter ...

When the bride's separated or divorced parents are hosts:
Mr David Murphy and Mrs Ann Murphy request the honour of your presence at the marriage of their daughter ...

When the bride's step-parent is the sole host:
Mr (or Mrs) Tom Hunt requests the honour of your presence at the marriage of his (or her) step-daughter ...

When a family member other than a parent hosts the wedding:

Mr and Mrs Michael Hanna request the honour of your presence at the marriage of their niece/cousin/granddaughter Kathleen Marie (last name can be included if different) ...

When a person who is no relation to the bride acts as host:
Mr and Mrs Tom Hardy request the honour of your presence at the marriage of Kathleen Marie Murphy ...

This wording may also be used if you are related, but choose not to specify the relationship.

CANCELLATION OR POSTPONEMENT

If the wedding is cancelled or postponed after the invitations have been posted, printed notices or handwritten cards should be sent immediately. If the invitations were formally printed, the cancellation or postponement notices should follow the same style.

Cancellation due to the death of a relative:
Owing to the recent death of her husband, Mrs Richard Harvey regrets that she is obliged to cancel the invitation to the marriage of her daughter Deirdre to Mr Larry Sykes, which will now take place quietly on 22nd May 1996.

Cancellation due to a broken engagement:
Mr and Mrs Richard Harvey announce that the marriage of their daughter Deirdre to Mr Larry Sykes will not now take place.

Postponement due to an illness in the family:
Owing to the illness of Mrs Douglas Sykes, Mr and Mrs Richard Harvey deeply regret that they are obliged to postpone the invitations to the marriage of their daughter Deirdre to Mr Larry Sykes at St Michael's Church, Belfast, from Friday, 19th August 1996 to Saturday, 3rd September 1996.

RECEPTION CARDS

Reception cards are similar to wedding invitations in style, paper, colour and printing. They are used when reception details are not given on the ceremony invitation or when the ceremony venue is too small to include everyone. The most frequently used form follows:

Mr and Mrs David Murphy
request the pleasure of your company
at a Reception to follow the Marriage of their
daughter Kathleen Marie
with Mr John Paul Kelly
at Green's Hotel, Ennis, County Clare
on Saturday, 28th July 1996
at 3.00 p.m.

6 Brookfield
Ennis, County Clare   RSVP

If the reception is to held at home, your invitation might read:

Mr and Mrs David Murphy
request the pleasure of the company of

_____

at a Reception
to follow the Marriage of their daughter
Kathleen Marie
with
Mr John Paul Kelly
on Saturday, 28th July 1996
to be held at home
at 3.00 p.m.

6 Brookfield
Ennis, County Clare   RSVP

EVENING ENCLOSURES

Evening enclosures are printed in the same style, colour and tone as
the ceremony invitation. They are used for inviting guests to join the
celebration once the wedding meal is finished — usually some hours
after the ceremony.

If the wedding is ultra-formal or formal and the bride's parents
are hosting the day, the invitation reads:

Mr and Mrs David Murphy
request the honour of your presence
at an evening reception to celebrate
the marriage of their daughter
Kathleen Marie with
Mr John Paul Kelly
at
Green's Hotel
Ennis, on Saturday, 28th July, 2 p.m.

6 Brookfield
Ennis, County Clare   RSVP

If the style of wedding is less formal and you are hosting the day you may prefer:

Kathleen and John Paul
have pleasure in inviting

_____

to share in the
celebration of their wedding at
Green's Hotel,
Ennis, County Clare
Saturday, 28th July, 1996
at 8.00 p.m.

6 Brookfield
Ennis, County Clare   RSVP

You may feel uncomfortable about inviting guests to the party only: if so a small explanatory note along the lines of the following can be included:

For a church wedding:
Due to the small size of St Michael's Church, only immediate family can be invited to the ceremony. We do hope you will join us for the celebration afterwards.

For a registry wedding:
Due to the small size of the Carlow Registry Office only immediate family can be invited to the ceremony. We do hope you will join us for the celebration afterwards.

Include a map with the invitation for out-of-town guests — a simple hand-drawn or photocopied map is all that is needed and it will be greatly appreciated.

ADDRESSING THE INVITATIONS AND ANNOUNCEMENTS

Ultra-formal invitations may come with two envelopes, an inner and an outer one. The inner envelope, which is not self-sealing, is placed inside the larger envelope so that the writing faces the flap. The writing should be neat and easy to read and written in blue or black ink only. If your handwriting is less than legible, try to find a friend or relative with particularly nice writing to help you, or, if you're willing to spend a little more money, hire a calligrapher.

Do not use abbreviations except for Mr, Mrs, and Dr. If a couple receiving the invitation are both doctors, use 'Dr' before each name, i.e. Dr Albert Tracey and Dr Jackie Tracey. Don't forget to use titles of profession such as The Honorable, The Reverend, or The Rabbi if appropriate.

On the inner envelope write only the guest's name:

Mr and Mrs Markle

On the outer envelope write the full name and address:

Mr and Mrs John Markle

921 Hall Park

Kilkenny

County Kilkenny

If the invitation is to a family, write their names on the inner envelope only. The outer envelope remains the same as above.

Mr and Mrs Markle

Teresa, John, Martin

When you invite someone who has a live-in partner or who is dating someone regularly, the partner should be invited as well:

Mr David Freeman

Ms Carolyn Curtis

or

David and Carolyn

If a guest would like to bring a date, write:

Ms Jennifer O'Beirne and Guest

A return address is written on the back flap or the upper lefthand corner of the outer envelope. Alternatively, the printer can engrave the address on the envelope, but this will cost more.

POSTAGE

Before buying stamps, take a completed sample invitation to the post office and ask the clerk to weigh it. Imagine how embarrassing it would be if your invitations were sent back to you or on to your guests with postage due.

RESPONSES

The best way to keep track of responses is by using the index cards described in Chapter 2. If your wedding day is getting very near and some guests have not responded, either of you or your parents, the chief bridesmaid or the best man should telephone for their response.

REPLYING TO AN INVITATION

A guest who receives an invitation without a response card should reply as follows:

Accepting:
Mr and Mrs Jonathan Smith have great pleasure in accepting the kind invitation of Mr and Mrs Charles Holly to the marriage of their daughter on Saturday, 2nd December, 1996, at All Saints Christian Church and afterwards at the Parker Hotel, Dingle.

Or
Jonathan and Margaret Smith are delighted to accept the invitation to your forthcoming wedding.

Declining:
Mr and Mrs Jonathan Smith thank Mr and Mrs Charles Holly for the kind invitation to the marriage of their daughter Deirdre but regret that they will be unable to accept.

STATIONERY PLANNER

Shop around to ensure you get a competitive estimate as prices vary. Call several printers and take note of their costs. Do not feel under any obligation to order more stationery than you need or can afford.

Estimate No. 1 Company _____

Address _____

Contact _____ Tel. _____

Envelopes	Number _____	Cost £ _____
Ceremony invitation	Number _____	Cost £ _____
Reception card	Number _____	Cost £ _____
Evening Invitations	Number _____	Cost £ _____
Reply card	Number _____	Cost £ _____
Order of Service book	Number _____	Cost £ _____
Place cards	Number _____	Cost £ _____
Napkins	Number _____	Cost £ _____
Napkin rings	Number _____	Cost £ _____
Matchboxes	Number _____	Cost £ _____
Cake boxes	Number _____	Cost £ _____
Envelope Seals	Number _____	Cost £ _____
Thank-you cards	Number _____	Cost £ _____
Other	Number _____	Cost £ _____

Total Cost £ _____ Deposit £ _____

Cancellation policy _____
_____

Estimate No. 2 Company _____

Address _____

Contact _____ Tel. _____

Envelopes	**Number** _____	**Cost £** _____
Ceremony invitation	Number _____	Cost £ _____
Reception card	Number _____	Cost £ _____
Evening Invitations	Number _____	Cost £ _____
Reply card	Number _____	Cost £ _____
Order of Service book	Number _____	Cost £ _____
Place cards	Number _____	Cost £ _____
Napkins	Number _____	Cost £ _____
Napkin rings	Number _____	Cost £ _____
Matchboxes	Number _____	Cost £ _____

Cake boxes	Number _____	Cost £ _____
Envelope Seals	Number _____	Cost £ _____
Thank-you cards	Number _____	Cost £ _____
Other	Number _____	Cost £ _____

Total Cost £ _____   Deposit £ _____

Cancellation policy _____

_____

Final Selection Company _____

Address _____

Contact _____   Tel. _____

Items ordered

Envelopes	Number _____	Cost £ _____
Ceremony invitation	Number _____	Cost £ _____
Reception card	Number _____	Cost £ _____
Evening Invitations	Number _____	Cost £ _____
Reply cards	Number _____	Cost £ _____
Order of Service book	Number _____	Cost £ _____
Place cards	Number _____	Cost £ _____
Napkins	Number _____	Cost £ _____
Napkin rings	Number _____	Cost £ _____
Matchboxes	Number _____	Cost £ _____
Cake boxes	Number _____	Cost £ _____
Envelope Seals	Number _____	Cost £ _____
Thank-you cards	Number _____	Cost £ _____
Other	Number _____	Cost £ _____

Total Cost £ _____   Deposit £ _____

Cancellation policy _____

_____

NOTES

13   WEDDING GIFTS

Within weeks of announcing your engagement a wonderful thing happens — friends and relatives begin sending you presents large and small. This is a tradition that has been a part of weddings as far back as anyone can remember and is an expression of the happiness and best wishes of those who know you.

As the recipients of such thoughtfulness, both of you should accept each gift graciously (even if it *is* your third toaster) and write a personal thank-you note as soon as possible. To save yourselves a great deal of confusion and embarrassment, it is helpful to make a note of each gift received, who sent it, and when a thank-you note was written. Use the gift organiser at the end of this chapter to keep track of gifts and thank-you notes.

If your wedding is very large, you may fall behind in sending thank-you letters. Don't panic. Ask your chief bridesmaid to help you send acknowledgement notes and follow up with a more personal letter within a month of your return from honeymoon.

WEDDING GIFT REGISTRY

If you have ever bought a present for someone else you know how difficult it is to pick out something that will really be needed and appreciated. Wedding presents are no different. Help guests find the ideal gift for you by registering your preferences at a department store, speciality shop or by using a bridal registry service. Far from thinking you forward, guests will be relieved to know exactly what you need.

A few years ago, bridal registry was almost unheard of in Ireland. Today most major shops offer wedding list services and will provide copies to your guests when they come in and choose a gift.

Begin by window shopping. Find one or two shops that sell goods you want and make a list of them, including the manufacturer's name, code number, your colour preference and quantities. Next, drop in or make an appointment to see the manager or person in charge of wedding lists. Some of the larger shops have staff specially trained to help you choose a selection and keep track of the items received. Alternatively, you may be given a gift book to fill out or be asked to leave a copy of your wedding list on file. Use the gift list at the end of this chapter.

It is a good idea to register for gifts in a wide range of prices so your friends are free to select one that fits their budget. Whenever possible, register in one shop for all your household needs as this makes shopping more convenient for others. Pop in to the stores or shops from time to time to go over the list. Be sure to strike off any gifts you have already received to avoid duplication (some shops offer this service as a courtesy).

So, now that you've registered, how do you let others know? Word of mouth is the best way and the most polite. Start by telling your families, wedding attendants and other friends. It is never proper to send a copy of your list to anyone other than your parents, chief bridesmaid and best man, and then only upon request. When friends ask what you would like, it is not polite to be specific so tell them where you are registered and let them know who to speak to there.

SETTING UP YOUR FIRST HOME

The following list represents the items you will probably need to set up your first home. It is meant as a guideline only as each couple's requirements will vary depending on their taste and circumstances.

Kitchenware	Dinner service	shakers
Baking dishes	Egg cups	Saucepans
Baking sheets	Frying pan	Scales
Cake tins	Glasses	Skillet
Can opener	Grater	Salad spinner
Carving knives	Juicer	Thermometer
Casserole dishes	Microwave	Timer
Coffeepot	Mixing Bowls	Toaster
Cookbooks	Ramekins	Utensils
Cutlery	Rolling pin	Wok
Cutting boards	Salt and pepper	Wooden spoons

Household
Hoover
Iron
Ironing board

Electronics
Hi-fi system
Clock radio
Television
VCR
Electric kettle
Food processor

Miscellaneous
Furniture
Garden furniture
Garden tools
Lamps
Luggage
Mirrors
Pictures
Rugs
Vases

Linens
Bedspread
Duvet
Duvet cover
Electric blanket
Pillows/ Pillow cases
Bathroom set
Towels

Stationery
Address book
Note paper
Visitor's book

DISPLAYING PRESENTS

As you receive wedding presents, you may wish to put them on display at home for friends and relatives to see when they come calling. Gifts should be arranged on a table away from any windows — no need to tempt would-be burglars. If you receive more than one of the same item, be considerate and display only one. For a pretty effect, cover a table with your best tablecloth and display one or two place settings of china or dishware with cutlery and crystal or glasses. Arrange other gifts by category (kitchen, bedroom, and bath, for example) or mix everything together for a dazzling display.

Money and other awkward or personal gifts (lingerie, very large items, etc) are better not displayed. Instead, type or neatly handwrite the giver's name and the gift on a sheet of clean white or pastel-coloured paper. In the case of money, never state the amount as it may cause embarrassment. When complete, leave the list on the table with your other gifts.

You may consider asking a trusted neighbour to watch over your gifts on your wedding day. Likewise, if the gifts are at your parents home, check with their insurance company about temporary extended coverage. Once the gifts are moved into your home, be sure that your own insurance is adequate.

EXCHANGING PRESENTS

Even if you register for presents, there is the possibility that one or two items may be duplicated. If you do not need the second gift, quietly exchange or return it but do not tell the giver as he or she may be quite embarrassed by the situation.

GIVING GIFTS

The joy of gifts is in giving as well as receiving so surprise each other, your parents, and your attendants with a small thank-you present on or before your wedding day. They can be token presents rather than anything grand, but should be a reminder of the event.

Ring holders, perfume bottles, picture frames, monogrammed handkerchiefs, silver boxes and small clocks make lovely gifts for the chief bridesmaid and other attendants. Money clips, flasks, pens, cufflinks and key chains are excellent presents for your best man and groomsmen. Your parents will probably love whatever you give them but a framed photo of the wedding couldn't fail to be appreciated.

Whether or not you buy gifts for one another will be a personal decision. Some couples like the idea of exchanging something special on or before their wedding day. Others prefer to pool their resources and get something they both want. Whatever you decide, talk it over first and if you choose to exchange presents, remember that this is an expensive time for both of you, so a very personal, small gift, chosen with care is best.

GIFTS AT THE RECEPTION

It is all too easy to lose track of gifts and cards at a reception, so assign a place where they can be secured. A locked cloakroom or changing room are fairly safe. Ask the best man, chief bridesmaid or other trusted friend to oversee the gifts and to be sure they are taken to your home after the wedding.

SENDING A GIFT

People who receive a wedding invitation usually send a gift, although giving one is not mandatory and you should never feel obliged to buy something extravagant or outside your budget.

Lovely wedding presents need not be expensive. A friend with a beautiful voice or a talent for sewing or baking might offer his or her services to the couple as a very special, personal gift. And a few friends could pool their funds to buy an expensive item they know a couple need. These type of gifts are always welcome and are a token of true affection.

Ideally, wedding presents should be sent to the bride or groom's home before the wedding. This saves everyone the hassle of bringing and safely storing the item on the day.

RETURNING WEDDING GIFTS

If for any reason the wedding is called off all presents should be returned to their senders with a brief note. Specific details need not be given. When the wedding has only been postponed and not cancelled, gifts may be kept unless after a reasonable amount of time the wedding does not take place. In a situation where one of the partners dies before the wedding takes place, it is only proper to keep those gifts which the giver strongly wishes you to have.

THANK-YOU LETTERS

A thank-you letter should be sent within a day or two of receiving a gift if possible. This is not a rule of etiquette but a good system of keeping on top of the task at hand. If you are lucky enough to be inundated with gifts, ask your mothers or bridesmaids for help, or send preprinted thank you notes. If you choose to do this, a handwritten, personal note should follow as soon as possible.

The letter need not be long, but it should be personal, even if you do not know the giver. Three or four thoughtful lines is plenty. Here are a few examples:

Dear Margaret,
Thank you for the lovely teapot which you dropped by yesterday. I'm sorry I was not here to open it with you personally, but Thomas and I opened it together when we got home. You'll be happy to know it suits our kitchen perfectly! Call in to us for a cuppa when you've time.
Love,
Orla

Dear Geraldine,

Many thanks for the beautiful silver picture frame. Thomas
and I have already filled it with a photo from our honeymoon
in Portugal. It looks great in the sitting room. Thank you for
thinking of us.

Love,

Orla

A you can see, neither note is particularly long, but both are warm
and friendly.

GIFT ORGANISER

Gift	Given by	Acknowledged

*'For I asked for a harder wedding gift than any woman ever asked before from
a man in Ireland — the absence of meanness and jealousy and fear.'*
— Queen Medbh of Connaught to her husband Ailill

GIFT LIST

Use these pages to help organise and keep track of your gift list:

FORMAL DINNERWARE			COOKING EQUIPMENT		
Pattern _____			Pattern _____		
Qty.	Item	Colour	Qty.	Item	Colour
____	____	_____	____	____	_____
____	____	_____	____	____	_____
____	____	_____	____	____	_____
____	____	_____	____	____	_____
____	____	_____	____	____	_____
____	____	_____	____	____	_____
____	____	_____	____	____	_____
____	____	_____	____	____	_____
____	____	_____	____	____	_____
____	____	_____	____	____	_____
____	____	_____	____	____	_____
____	____	_____	____	____	_____
____	____	_____	____	____	_____
____	____	_____	____	____	_____

EVERYDAY GLASSWARE			CRYSTAL		
Pattern _____			Pattern _____		
Qty.	Item	Colour	Qty.	Item	Colour
____	____	_____	____	____	_____
____	____	_____	____	____	_____
____	____	_____	____	____	_____
____	____	_____	____	____	_____
____	____	_____	____	____	_____
____	____	_____	____	____	_____
____	____	_____	____	____	_____
____	____	_____	____	____	_____
____	____	_____	____	____	_____
____	____	_____	____	____	_____
____	____	_____	____	____	_____
____	____	_____	____	____	_____
____	____	_____	____	____	_____
____	____	_____	____	____	_____
____	____	_____	____	____	_____
____	____	_____	____	____	_____
____	____	_____	____	____	_____
____	____	_____	____	____	_____

CUTLERY
Pattern _____

Qty.	Item	Colour

LINENS
Pattern _____

Qty.	Item	Colour

EVERYDAY DISHWARE
Pattern _____

Qty.	Item	Colour

MISCELLANEOUS ITEMS
Pattern _____

Qty.	Item	Colour

14   PRE-WEDDING PARTIES

One reason a wedding is so much fun is that there is so much to celebrate: the engagement party, the hen and stag party and the biggest event of all — the reception. It's a busy time — make sure you enjoy it. The trick with pre-wedding parties is to be creative but not fussy. Instead of trying to organise a three-course meal, invite everyone over for a barbecue or Chinese takeaway, get in some beer and use paper plates and disposable forks to save time cleaning up afterwards.

Even though wedding parties are less traditional these days, there are still a few rules of etiquette attached. You are, of course, free to accept or decline the invitation of friends and relatives who offer to host a party for you. If you have more than one party, your guests should not be expected to bring a gift every time and both of you should quietly point this out to your friends. If someone does host a party for you, write a thank-you note within a week.

BRIDAL SHOWERS

Hen parties are increasingly known as 'bridal showers' — a name which has its origins in an old European tradition about a poor miller's daughter who longed to marry her true love but couldn't because her father disapproved of him and wouldn't provide the necessary dowry. Friends of the couple in their village 'showered' them with all the riches needed for the bride's dowry and the happy couple married.

Contemporary bridal showers have changed radically from the days of the all-female hen party. Nowadays, many women have a female equivalent of the stag party — a meal or drinks followed by a night on the town — or take up a theme idea, some of which even include men! Why not try one of these:

AROUND-THE-CLOCK SHOWER

Guests are assigned a time of day and they bring a gift which the couple might need at that hour. A guest with 8a.m., for example, might give coffee cups or a selection of coffees and teas. Someone assigned 1p.m. might give a thermos flask or picnic basket. Another person with 10p.m. might bring a candle or nightlight, and so on.

BAR SHOWER

A bar shower is geared towards future parties! Guests give anything that the couple might need for entertaining. For example, a group of friends might pitch in and buy a beautiful punchbowl or microwave. Or a friend might bring a cheeseboard, glasses, a wine rack, drink mats, an ice bucket, a jug or a fondue set.

KITCHEN SHOWER

Guests bring gifts that turn the couple's kitchen into a gourmet's paradise. An electric kettle, coffee machine, wok, mixer, toaster, pots and pans, baking dishes, cutlery, glasses, dishes, pot holders, dishcloths, tea cosy, can opener, fun magnets for the fridge, or a cookbook would all be suitable.

LINGERIE SHOWER

This is particularly fun when there is a good mix of men and women. Friends bring anything from silk boxers to slippers, and the couple take turns opening them. Catch the groom opening things like the teddies, camisoles, and lacy underwear!

LINEN SHOWER

Linen can be expensive for newly weds so a linen shower is perfect for those just setting up home. Possible gifts include towels, napkins, tablecloths, bedspread, duvet, dishcloths, pillowcases, or bath mats.

THE STAG PARTY

A stag party is an all-male affair thrown in honour of the groom by his best man: sometimes it is referred to as the 'bachelor party'. Friends of the groom, his male attendants and both fathers are usually invited, though the fathers generally stay only for the first few rounds of drink, leaving 'the boys' to their own shenanigans.

Traditionally, the party is given the night before the wedding but, these days, it is much wiser to organise it for at least a week beforehand. Many a groom has woken from a night of heavy drinking to find himself hundreds of miles from home or wrapped unnecessarily in plaster!

There are ways to make this a more enjoyable party for everyone. For instance, start the day off with a good game of golf, football or tennis, or organise an afternoon of Skirmish. Let everyone get home for a quick shower, then meet up for a meal and head off to the pub, the theatre, or a nightclub. One word of advice: assign someone to drive, or hire a coach — this is meant to be a fun night.

BRIDESMAIDS' LUNCH

A bridesmaids' lunch is an American custom which would transfer well to this country. The month before the wedding the bride usually hosts a lunch or tea in her house (or her parents' house) for her bridesmaids as a gesture of thanks and appreciation for their support. Mothers are often invited too.

The setting is relaxed and should give the bride and her friends the chance to chat. Sandwiches, salads, warm scones, quiche, petits fours, fresh fruit and a variety of teas or wine are perfect for this gathering. After the meal, the bride generally gives thank-you gifts to her attendants. While she is doing so, a sponge cake is presented which involves another tradition. Baked into the cake is a thimble or small, inexpensive ring and the woman who finds it in her piece of cake is supposed to be next to marry.

REHEARSAL DINNER

Another international tradition which you may wish to borrow is the rehearsal dinner. This usually follows the ceremony rehearsal and is hosted by the groom's family. It is an informal meal — one where the bridal party and your families have a chance to relax and get to know one another better.

The dinner should be easy to prepare — a big pot of spaghetti, a barbecue or pizza are perfect. The party is usually at the home of the groom's parents or a favourite restaurant though sometimes the setting is more exotic, such as a barge, yacht club or outdoor picnic. Guests generally bring spouses or steady partners.

The best part of the night is the speeches. Unlike the wedding reception, the speeches at the rehearsal are impromptu. The best man usually starts by telling some funny stories about his friend and finishes by saying something nice about the couple. The chief bridesmaid also gets a chance to say something. Then the floor is open to anyone who wants to get up and speak.

PARTY FOR VISITING GUESTS

Friends and relatives who live far away sometimes make a special effort to return for a couple's wedding day. Let them know how much you appreciate their arrival by organising a get-together or party in their honour. A picnic at the beach, brunch at home, or a meal at a local restaurant are but a few suggestions. If time allows, a breakfast the morning after the wedding is another good way to bring everybody together before they depart.

Brides, lads and young lasses can there fill their glasses
With whiskey and send a full bumper round;
Jig it off in the tent till their money is spent,
And spin like a top till they rest on the ground.
From a ballad about Donnybrook Fair.

PARTY PLANNER

Use this page to keep track of pre-wedding party plans.

Host/Hostess _____

Date _____ Time _____ No. of guests _____

Address _____

Theme _____

Food _____
_____

Drinks _____
_____

Guest list

_____
_____
_____
_____
_____
_____
_____
_____

Host/Hostess _____

Date _____ Time _____ No. of guests _____

Address _____

Theme _____

Food _____
_____

Drinks _____
_____

Guest list

_____
_____
_____
_____
_____
_____
_____

15   BLOOMING EVERYWHERE

Flowers are a funny thing. Few couples can imagine their wedding without flowers and yet if you ask someone who has recently been to a wedding what they remember about the floral arrangements, they can rarely give a detailed answer. They will probably remember whether the flowers were beautiful or dreadful but they won't be able to say what blooms or colours were used, or how they were arranged.

The point is that although flowers add atmosphere, they are not all-important. It won't matter to your guests whether the church appears to be blooming everywhere or whether it is decorated with a few well-chosen arrangements. What does matter is their meaning to you. Try incorporating flowers which hold an important memory for you. If she always gave you a yellow rose on special occasions, wear one in your lapel. If the first time he kissed you was under the mistletoe, try including some in your bouquet. Flowers can carry personal messages too. Use them on your wedding day to say something, if not to everyone present, then privately to each other.

THE TRADITION OF FLOWERS

Flowers and weddings have been closely linked since before the time of Christ. In ancient Rome, garlands of wheat were worn by the bride and groom to ensure a fertile union. It was in medieval times that brides first wore wreaths of real flowers in their hair. No flower, however, is as closely associated with weddings as the orange blossom. Saracen brides during the tenth century wore this fragrant bloom, and the custom travelled from Syria to Europe at the end of the Crusades and westwards in the nineteenth century to the Americas.

Like the shaft of wheat, the orange blossom symbolised fertility, but, because of its delicate white flowers, it also stood for beauty. Perhaps part of its popularity grew out of a romantic twelfth-century legend about the king of Spain. The king's gardener grew a beautiful tree which in spring was full of white fragrant blooms and in summer bore sweet fruit. An ambassador from the French court visited the king and thought the tree was truly remarkable. He asked the king for a cutting to take back to his country, but the king wanted to keep the tree a secret and refused. Meanwhile, the gardener's daughter was deeply in love. However, because she had no dowry she could not marry. She stole a cutting from the orange tree and gave it to the French ambassador in exchange for gold and other riches. As a symbol of her appreciation to the tree, she wore orange blossoms in her hair on her wedding day.

Until recently, it was customary to use only white flowers — carnations, roses, lilies and orchids — for weddings. But now, colour is making an appearance, a shower bouquet of stargazer lilies, for example, pink and cream roses, freesia, alstromaria and gypsophilia, a single gerbera tied with a matching bow, or a bundle of gypsophilia wrapped in satin.

THE LANGUAGE OF FLOWERS

In Victorian times, the language of flowers was very fashionable. Up to then flowers had held symbolic and mythological significance, but in the early nineteenth century Mme Charlotte de la Tour wrote the first flower dictionary, *Le Language des Fleurs*, which assigned each flower a meaning. And though the meaning of each flower has changed today, the idea still holds.

The following is a list of commonly used flowers and their meanings — try incorporating one or two in your own arrangements.

Almond Blossom: *Hope*

Apple Blossom: *Good fortune*

Azalea: *Temperance*

Camellia: *Perfect loveliness*

Carnation: *Fascination*

Chrysanthemum (red): *Sharing*

Chrysanthemum (white): *Truth*

Daisy: *Innocence*

Fern: *Sincerity*

Forget-me-not: *True love*

Gardenia: *Joy*

Geranium: *True friendship*

Heather: *Luck*

Hibiscus: *Delicate beauty*

Honeysuckle: *Devotion*

Iris: *Burning love*

Ivy: *Fidelity, friendship and marriage*

Jasmine: *Grace*

Lily: *Purity*

Lily of the Valley: *Happiness*

Myrtle: *Love*

Orchid: *Beauty*

Orange Blossom: *Fertility*

Rose: *Love*

Snowdrop: *Hope*

Tulip: *Love*

Violet: *Faithfulness*

Another Victorian custom you might borrow spells out the name of your future spouse with flowers. Carnations, almond blossom, roses and lilies spell Carl, for example, while primrose, anemone and tulip spell Pat.

BRINGING IN A PROFESSIONAL

Flowers, like so many other wedding details, reflect the tone of the ceremony and reception. Though there are no rules on the kind of flowers or number of arrangements, you should pick up a colour theme and style that echoes that of your wedding outfit and those of your bridal party. But because there are so many flowers and designs to choose from — and a budget to consider — it may be worthwhile seeking the help of an expert. And this can be done once the bride's gown has been chosen.

If you do decide to hire a florist, book him or her three to four months before the wedding day, if possible. (If your wedding is near Christmas, Valentine's Day or another special day, you may need to book five to six months ahead.) It may seem strange to interview a florist but this is important. The person who does your flowers should have a real understanding of the mood you're trying to create. Don't be content to settle for the first florist you find unless he or she truly understands what you want.

The first thing the florist will need to know is how much you wish to spend. This decision should be made before you meet as it is easy to get carried away and spend more than you originally planned. The tradition is that the groom pays for all flowers carried by the bride, her attendants, the flower girl, both mothers, the best man, ushers or groomsmen, both fathers, the ring bearer, readers, honorary guests — as well as his own — while the bride's family pays for all other arrangements.

Once you have chosen a florist, be more specific about what you want — show him or her swatches of fabric from the bride's and bridesmaids' dresses, a photo or sketch of the gowns and any magazine photos you may have seen and liked. Mention any flower that has a special meaning for your relationship so that, if possible, it can be incorporated into the arrangements.

A good florist should have photographs of arrangements, bouquets, baskets, buttonholes, etc., on hand for your perusal. He or she should also have recommendations and be willing to share the tricks of the trade. For instance, if you want to accentuate a thin waist or disguise a not so thin one, the florist should be able to help!

Lastly, ask for a rough estimate in writing. This should include the date and time of the wedding, an address and time of delivery, a list of all the arrangements to be used and a design or delivery fee. If a deposit is required, be sure to ask about refunds just in case.

THE FIRST STEP

Whether you are employing a florist or doing your own flowers, the first step in organising flowers for your wedding day is to decide what is needed. For the ceremony you'll probably want a bridal bouquet, bridesmaids' bouquets, a basket or other small arrangement for the flower girl, and buttonholes for the groom, best man, groomsmen, ushers, and ring bearer. Don't forget buttonholes for fathers and brothers and perhaps for grandfathers, and corsages or single blooms for mothers, sisters and grandmothers. You might also like flower arrangements for the altar or the registry office, seat or pew decorations, as well as a second bouquet for tossing.

For the reception, you may need flowers to present to your mothers during the speeches, for the top table and the buffet tables and for other key places like the entrance to the venue. If there is a sit-down meal, you may want flowers for each table. Remember to make sure the flower arrangements are low so that they don't interfere with conversation across the tables. If the reception is at a hotel or club ask the banqueting manager if flowers are included as part of their service — most do so at no extra cost.

CUTTING COSTS

Even if you are planning a wedding on a small budget, beautiful flowers are still possible. Avoid busy times such as Christmas and Valentine's Day, when the price of flowers increases. Don't use exotic blooms or large arrangements. Instead ask about locally grown flowers or those in season. Consider using lots of greenery and a few bold flowers such as lilies, roses or orchids. Or be dramatic and carry a single bloom, perhaps a bird of paradise, longiflorum or gerbera.

Between April and September there can be as many as three couples marrying in the same church over a number of days. Ask your clergy about other weddings within two days of yours — the couples may be interested in sharing the cost of ceremony flowers. Some churches have a floral committee or parishioners who look after the flowers regularly. Quite often they are willing to design wedding arrangements for a small donation or fee.

If you are planning a reception at home, bring the ceremony flowers to the house. Be sure to assign a trusted friend to move the flowers with enough time to set them up before guests arrive. Consider using potted plants which can be given to guests or planted in your own garden later.

Perhaps the most effective way to keep down costs is to arrange them yourself. Your own garden may have a variety of flowers and greenery to fill delightful bouquets and arrangements. Some of the flowers you might find in your garden or local florist include:

Spring: anemone; carnation; cherry blossom; daffodil; freesia; gypsophelia; hyacinth; jasmine; lilac; lily of the valley; narcissus; orange blossom; orchid; polyanthus; primrose; tulip

Summer: aster; carnation; chrysanthemum; cornflower; daisy; delphinium; freesia; fuschia; gladioli; lily; marigold; peony; rose; sweet william; stock; sweet pea

Autumn: chrysanthemum; dahlia; freesia; gypsophelia; hydrangea; morning glory

Winter: anemone; azalea; carnation; chrysanthemum; freesia; gladiolus; gypsophelia; orchid; snowdrop; heather; winter jasmine

All year round: aucuba japonica; box; carnation; fern; freesia; gypsophelia; hebe; iris; ivy; lily; mistletoe; orchid; reed grass; rose; skimmia japonica; spray chrysanthemum

DRIED FLOWERS

If you want your flowers to last indefinitely have your arrangements made with silk or dried flowers. Both come in a wide variety of colours and are more durable, and sometimes less expensive, than the real thing. Christmas is a particularly good time to use dried flowers as there is a wider selection available, usually at cheaper rates. Both silk and dried flowers are available from florists and dried flower specialists around the country.

FLOWERS FOR THE WEDDING PARTY

Bridal bouquets usually come in four shapes: single bloom, posy, hand tied and cascading. The single bloom makes a dramatic statement and is generally carried across the length of the arm from elbow to hand (a Gerbera or Bird of Paradise are simple and elegant). A posy can be large or small and is a somewhat dome shaped arrangement put into a plastic handle for easy carrying. Hand tied bouquets are round but very natural looking because the stems are tied together and then wrapped in satin ribbon. A cascading or shower bouquet is tightly bundled at the top and flows downward elegantly.

SINGLE BLOOM

POSY

HAND TIED

CASCADING

The flower for the groom's buttonhole usually matches the bride's bouquet. White carnations or roses are popular, but, for a change, consider using irises, coloured roses or carnations, orchids or a combination of several flowers with greenery. Fern, purple heather and a pink or white rose make a beautiful buttonhole.

The other men in your bridal party — including the ring bearer, fathers, brothers, grandfathers, and other special guests — should also have a buttonhole but this should be slightly different, perhaps being a different colour or bloom, to the groom's buttonhole. For example, if the bride's bouquet is of orchids, pink roses and white carnations and freesia, the groom's buttonhole could be a single orchid with greenery, the best man and other male attendants could sport buttonholes of pink rose and gypsophelia, the ring bearer could wear freesia and greenery, while the fathers and special guests could have a single white carnation.

Bouquets for the bridesmaids should also complement the style and colour of the bride's flowers. Occasionally, the chief bridesmaid may carry different flowers from the other bridesmaids.

Flower girls normally carry a small posy or basket of petals which can be strewn outside the entrance of the church or registry office after the ceremony. But do check that your clergy or registrar has no objections before you organise this. Confetti is usually frowned upon, so ask about using a combination of dried rose petals and birdseeds — both are environmentally friendly and don't need to be cleaned up.

A corsage or single flower is perfect for mothers, sisters, grandmothers and other special female guests. These flowers — and those for your fathers, brothers and grandfathers — should be delivered to them early on the day of the wedding, or sent directly to the church.

If a loved one has recently passed away, you may wish to take a bouquet of flowers to the grave after the ceremony and before arriving to the reception. You may, of course, leave your bridal bouquet or, if you prefer, have a second, specially made bouquet for this touching custom.

Lastly, the bride may want to wear a corsage on her going away outfit and the groom may like a matching buttonhole. These can be built into the bride's bouquet and removed just before it is tossed.

FOR THE RECEPTION

Generally, most restaurants or hotels provide flowers for the reception as part of their service, so you only need to arrange flowers if you are having a reception at home. Flowers for the reception need not be the same as the bridal flowers. They should, however, complement the colour of the bride's and bridesmaids' dresses. Take the time to discuss with the hotel or catering staff where the flowers and table decorations will be placed.

For an at-home reception, position the flowers for greatest impact — near the door where you will be receiving your guests is a good place. Flowers on a buffet table tend to get in the way unless they are placed in the centre of the table with the food arranged around them. Never put tall floral arrangements on the top table as they tend to obscure your guests' view.

Another touching custom is to present your mothers with flowers at the reception. Just after the groom makes his speech is a good time for the bride to bring an arrangement to her mother, while the groom carries flowers to his mother.

PRESERVING YOUR BOUQUET

If you want to preserve your wedding bouquet and buttonhole, you can have them professionally done or do so yourself. First refrigerate the flowers after the wedding and ask someone else to begin the process within twenty-four hours if you are going away on honeymoon. For home preservation, choose one of the following:

Air drying: Take arrangement apart. Remove all leaves from stems and tie each variety of flower together with string or rubber bands. Hang tied bunches upside down in a cool dry place for one month. When flowers are dried, arrange as before.

Framing: This method requires a little more work but makes a lovely memento to hang on a wall. Carefully take your bouquet apart. Lay each flower and piece of greenery flat on a sheet of newspaper, making sure they don't touch each other. Cover with two sheets of newspaper and put a heavy book on top. Leave to press in a cool dry room. Two months later rearrange flowers on matting and frame with glass.

Pot Pourri: Remove petals from flowers and lay on baking sheet in one layer. When petals are completely dried mix with cinnamon, allspice, cloves, orange peel, lemon geranium, marjoram, lavender and one teaspoon of oris root (for every two cups of dried petals) or a few drops from any aromatic oil. Store in sealed glass jar for three weeks, shaking regularly.

FLORAL ORGANISER

Estimate No 1: Company _____

Contact _____ Tel. _____

Delivery _____

Cancellation policy _____

_____

Cost £ _____ Deposit £ _____

Estimate No 2: Company _____

Contact _____ Tel. _____

Delivery _____

Cancellation policy _____

_____

Cost £ _____ Deposit £ _____

Estimate No 3: Company _____

Contact _____ Tel. _____

Delivery _____

Cancellation policy _____

_____

Cost £ _____ Deposit £ _____

Final Selection: Company _____

Contact _____

Address _____ Tel. _____

Delivery _____

Flowers ordered _____

_____

_____

Cancellation policy _____

_____

Cost £ _____ Deposit £ _____

NOTES

16   THE SOUND OF MUSIC

From the first resounding chord to the last swinging beat, the music you select for your ceremony and reception is a vital element in setting the tone and mood for your wedding day. It is also a chance to include the pieces of music that have a special significance for you and your relationship. Even so, in the bustle of planning a wedding, music is a powerful detail which is often overlooked. If neither of you knows very much about music, take some time to research the subject together.

THE CEREMONY

Music at the ceremony should enhance the mood you wish to create. A large, formal, traditional marriage calls for sacred or classical arrangements, usually featuring an organ, trained soloist, choir or combination of the three. A more relaxed or informal celebration is generally lighter in tone and incorporates congregational singing, a folk group, string quartet, Irish harp, organ or piano. Make an appointment with the officiant, early on, to find out what guidelines must be followed and at what stage during the ceremony music is appropriate. In a church wedding, it is customary to have music with the processional (the bride's entrance), the Communion (if it is being celebrated), the signing of the register and the recessional (your exit). To help you decide, ask your celebrant for suggestions, and borrow Order of Service or Mass booklets from other weddings.

Your officiant may suggest a resident musician, choir or organist who has probably played for many weddings. This is an option worth considering, but before you decide, meet the musician to talk over some ideas. If possible, attend a Mass or ceremony where he or she is playing. There's no better way to make a decision than to hear the music yourself.

If you decide another musician or choir would be more to your liking, you must get permission from your clergy in case there are some restrictions of which you are not aware. In many cases, you will be required to pay a fee to the resident musician even if you do not avail of his or her services. If your budget is tight, this alone may cause you to rethink your decision. If a talented friend or relative is willing, you might consider asking them to look after the music. They will probably be delighted and they might like to make it their wedding gift — so saving you the expense!

Music can be a very special part of a registry office wedding because it allows a couple to put a personal stamp on the ceremony. As with church services, music may accompany the bride's entrance, the signing of the register and the conclusion of the ceremony. You should make enquiries at your local registry office for more specific details on the type of music allowed and space limitations. In general, registry offices do not supply music but you may be allowed to bring taped music or an instrumentalist such as a harpist or violinist.

If you are still at a loss for music, try your local music shop or library. The sales assistant or librarian will usually help you sift through the many religious, classical and modern selections suitable for weddings. Some music shops carry sheet music which is appropriate for weddings. Again, consult your clergy or officiant after you have made your decisions. Many religions have rules pertaining to music and some may not allow secular music.

If you want to reprint the hymns you have chosen in your Order of Service book, you need to contact the publisher of the piece to ask for permission. Generally, this is a formality and no fee is required as long as you print an acknowledgement in the book.

Plan to attend at least one music session before the wedding so that you know the quality of the instrument(s) and/or voice(s) and the mood the music creates. If you do not like the pieces the organist has selected don't hesitate to say so — as long as this is discussed early on, there is plenty of time for change.

BEFORE THE CEREMONY

The first few selections are usually pieces the organist has chosen to play while guests are arriving, generally for about half an hour before the ceremony begins. This music is usually joyful but not overbearing. *Arioso* by Bach, *Love is his Word* by Luke Connaughton and Anthony Milnert, and *Bí Íosa im' Chroíse*, are some suggestions. As this is also when the groom is waiting anxiously for the arrival of his bride, it is nice to include some of his favourite music here. Just before the bride comes in, the music generally pauses and a change of mood marks her entrance. Organ music is the usual choice for the processional, although a trumpet solo or hymn sung by a choir is equally dramatic. Other possibilities include:

> *Adagio* by Mozart
> *Ag an bPósadh 'bhí i gCana*
> *Irish Lullaby* by J.R. Shannon
> *Trumpet Voluntary* by Clarke

BRIDE'S ENTRANCE

The processional piece should have a rhythm that is easy for the bride and her father to walk down the aisle to. When you hold the wedding rehearsal, invite the musicians so you can practice together — most of the bridal party will need to know exactly how many verses it takes to walk down the aisle. All too often, embarrassing mishaps occur during this part of the ceremony. Consider one of the following:

> *Trumpet Voluntary* by Clarke or Purcell
> *Air* from the *The Water Music* by Handel
> *Opening Fanfare* from *Te Deum* by Charpentier
> *Wedding March* from *The Marriage of Figaro* by Mozart
> *The Arrival of the Queen of Sheba* by Handel
> *Pomp and Circumstance* by Elgar
> *Bridal Chorus* by Wagner (also known as *Here Comes the Bride*)
> *Rigaudon* by Campra
> *Largo* from *Xerxes* by Handel

SIGNING OF THE REGISTER

The signing of the register is a perfect time for a musical interlude as this is a natural break in the ceremony. Often this is a good place for romantic classical or popular music, but do check first with your celebrant before using any non-religious music. If there is a problem, you may get the go-ahead if you stick with the instrumental version rather than including the vocalists. Whether you have an organist, string quartet, soloist or choir is up to you but keep in mind that the performer will probably be the focus of your guests' attention so the music should be well rehearsed. Some suitable pieces include:

Sheep May Safely Graze by Bach
Ave Maria by Bach
Jesu, Joy of Man's desiring by Bach
To a Wild Rose by MacDowell
Air from the *The Water Music* by Handel
Adagio in G Minor by Mozart
How Lovely is thy Dwelling Place by Brahms
Minuet from *Berenice* by Handel
Hymn to Love by David Julien and Pamela Stotter
Deus Meus Adiuva Mé by Maol Íosa Ó Brolcháin
Spiorad Dé by Máire Ní Dhuibhir
Ag an bPósadh 'bhí i gCana

RECESSIONAL

The recessional is the grand finale of the wedding ceremony and the music you choose should reflect the jubilant spirit of the occasion. Quite a lot of the music suggested for the bride's entrance would be equally good for the joyous exit. Whatever piece you decide upon should be long enough to allow you both to walk down the aisle and go outside. Any one of the following is lovely:

Fugue in C Minor by Buxtehude
Canon in D Major by Pachebel
Trumpet Tune by Purcell or Stanley
Toccata by Widor or Buxtehude
Grand March from *Aida* by Verdi
Wedding March from *A Midsummer Night's Dream* by Mendelssohn
Ode to Joy from *Symphony No. 9* by Beethoven
Music for the Royal Fireworks by Handel
Trumpet Voluntary by Clarke
The Ride of the Valkyrie by Wagner

Once the couple and wedding party are down the aisle, *Nun Danket alle Gott* by Karl-Elert is super for the departure of guests. It is a strong, flowing piece, wonderful for the end of a wedding.

If you are marrying in the Church of Ireland, be sure to ask your vicar about organising bellringers for the recessional. There is nothing more romantic than the sound of pealing churchbells at the end of a wedding ceremony.

These are just a few possibilities and are meant to outline only the very basic moments during the ceremony when music may be played. Other suitable times may include communion, responsorial psalms, the marriage and candle ceremony, and the offertory. Talk to your celebrant, as he or she can give you a better idea of when music is appropriate and may be able to suggest other suitable pieces.

THE RECEPTION

Continue the festive mood at the reception by arranging to have some live or recorded music played while drinks are served or photographs are taken. The music itself should be uplifting but soft and unobtrusive. Guests should be able to talk to one another without having to shout. When the bride and groom enter the reception, special music could be used such as *Love Changes Everything* by Andrew Lloyd Weber, *O'Carolan's Concerto* by Turlough O'Carolan or *Theme from Love Story* by F. Lai.

Nowadays many people like to use traditional Irish music during the reception: some suggestions are *She Moved through the Fair*, *Danny Boy*, *Gortnamona*, *The Spinning Wheel* by Walter and Murphy, *Carrick-fergus*, or music by Thomas Moore such as *Love thee dearest*, *The Last Rose of Summer*, *Oft in the Stilly Night* or *Down by the Sally Gardens*.

If you are having a small gathering at home, taped music or a single instrument such as a pianist, flautist, or harpist is perfect. When space is limited but you would like a larger group, opt for a three-piece group such as two violinists and a cellist.

For an outdoor reception at home, a string quartet or steel band makes lovely background music. If you are hiring a band to perform outdoors, be sure there are enough power sockets, some form of shelter in the case of rain and room for the musicians to set up their instruments and play comfortably.

FINDING A BAND

Many musicians do not advertise. They rely on word of mouth or their manager to make their bookings. Start your search by asking friends, family and co-workers for their suggestions. If you attend a wedding or party with a great band, introduce yourself to them during their break and ask for their phone number. The *Golden Pages* is another good resource — look under 'Musicians' or 'Bands' — as are music agencies which are also found in the phone book. Agencies are great for trying to locate speciality bands such as jazz, céilí, reggae or calypso. That said, they do charge a fee which is incorporated into the total price, and to save money you are better hiring a band directly. To find a céilí band, the organisation for Irish folk music, Comhaltas Ceoltóirí Éireann are a good resource. (Contact Seamus MacMathúna on 01-2800295 for advice and assistance.) If your reception is at a hall, hotel, restaurant or club, ask the banqueting manager whether they have a resident musician.

The cost of a band varies depending on several things: experience, popularity, number of musicians involved, whether they have to learn new music, time required and distance travelled. On average, you can expect to pay between £150 and £600 for a good group. When you consider all the factors involved, it's money well spent.

Once you have a list of possibilities, contact the group's agent or manager to get a copy of their current song list. If you have a preference for a certain type of music, reviewing the list can help you eliminate those who do not meet your requirements. Next, go and hear the group perform. Keep an eye on their attitude, professionalism and dress. A good musician should be versatile enough to cater to dancers and listeners alike and be comfortable playing a range of songs. Check their volume too. An over-loud group is just as unpleasant as one you cannot hear. Lastly, ask for references and follow them up.

When you reach a decision, get your agreement with the band in writing. The agent or manager may try to put you off this idea, but it is worth insisting. Outline when the musicians will arrive, how long they will play, number and length of breaks, and agree on payment and deposit (often a band prefers to be paid in cash on the night). Find out if they would be willing to play later, and if so at what cost. And if you have time, make out a rough list of songs you would like them to play. It is also a good idea to detail any special requests — the music for the first dance, tossing the garter, cutting the cake, etc. You should be very clear about the group's cancellation policy. On more than one occasion a lead singer has fallen ill, the band has gotten lost, or the wrong details were provided and ruined a couple's wedding day. A cancellation or refund policy may not help you on the day, but it may prevent you having to pay full price for a service unfulfilled. Finally, make sure the band knows whether they should wear black tie or jeans and jumpers.

MUSIC FOR THE CEREMONY

Estimate No. 1: Company _____

Contact _____ Tel. _____

Arrival time _____ Playing time _____

Cancellation policy _____

_____

Cost £ _____ Deposit £ _____

Estimate No. 2: Company _____

Contact _____ Tel. _____

Arrival time _____ Playing time _____

Cancellation policy _____

_____

Cost £ _____ Deposit £ _____

Estimate No. 3: Company _____

Contact _____ Tel. _____

Arrival time _____ Playing time _____

Cancellation policy _____

_____

Cost £ _____ Deposit £ _____

Final Selection: Company _____

Contact _____ Tel. _____

Arrival time _____ Playing time _____

Cancellation policy _____

_____

Cost £ _____ Deposit £ _____ Balance due £ _____

Choice of Music: Prelude _____

_____

Processional _____

_____

During ceremony _____

_____

_____

Recessional _____

_____

MUSIC FOR THE RECEPTION

Estimate No. 1: Company

Contact	Tel.
Arrival time	Playing time
Cancellation policy	

Cost £   Deposit £

Estimate No. 2: Company

Contact	Tel.
Arrival time	Playing time
Cancellation policy	

Cost £   Deposit £

Estimate No. 3: Company

Contact	Tel.
Arrival time	Playing time
Cancellation policy	

Cost £   Deposit £

Final Selection: Company

Contact	Tel.
Arrival time	Playing time
Cancellation policy	

Cost £   Deposit £   Balance due £

Special Announcements:

Requests:

NOTES

17 MEMORIES FOR A LIFETIME

Your wedding day is a once in a lifetime celebration and you will want to mark the occasion with high quality photographs and, if you choose, an equally good video. To make sure your memories last a lifetime, choose professionals with great care and a little research. Start by asking friends and family for the names of people they have hired in the past. If you are at a complete loss, the *Golden Pages* and the Irish Professional Photographers' Association are two good sources.

Once you have drawn up a list of possibilities, telephone each one and make an appointment with the photographer or videographer to see samples of their work. Ask to be shown complete wedding albums or videos. Look to see that the mood and spirit of the couple have been captured. If every shot looks the same, the photographer has not done a great job — just a good one.

Photographs should be clear and varied. Did the photographer vary the background, shoot from different angles, arrange imaginative poses, cover the entire day, take group shots? Is the video image clear, camera steady, sound track appropriate? Are the scenes flattering and is the finale strong? If not, it is a sure sign that the videographer lacks creativity or is not up to date with the latest trends and techniques.

Be forewarned, wedding photography and videography are expensive. This is not because industry professionals are taking advantage of a couple's need, but because the business is labour intensive. The fee you pay covers the photographer's time and expertise, in addition to film stock, lab processing or post-production work, an album or jacket cover, and possibly an assistant on the day.

If you are considering asking a friend to take pictures or hiring a photographer whose reputation is unknown to you, be very sure you will be happy with the results first. Once the wedding is over you cannot go back and recapture the memories.

Talk with each professional at length before making your decision. Photographs and videos are an extension of yourselves and the person hired to capture the day should know almost intuitively what you might consider special or important. If you are not being understood, or the chemistry is not there, it is definitely time to contact someone else.

Once you have viewed the professional's work, and are satisfied it is good, ask specific questions. Find out who will be the photographer and whether there will be an assistant on hand. Is there a lot of equipment involved? How many photos do you get for the quote, and do you get copies of every picture taken or only the ones they think are good? Have they got back-up equipment in the event of a problem? Can they come to your house early in the day to get pre-wedding shots, and how many other weddings do they have arranged for that day? Where is the editing done? Is post-production work made to specification? Can you select the music dub-ins? How long is the video? Ask about the cost of proofs or contact sheets and whether the quote includes the finished album or video? Are any package or all-inclusive deals on offer? Is a deposit necessary in advance?

The number of photographs in your album can vary. Some photographers will require you to select an album when you pay the deposit which limits you to a fixed number of pictures. Others are more flexible, allowing you to pick the album and the number of photos when you see the results. On average you can expect to pay between £300 and £700 for approximately twenty-four photos.

Once you have reached an agreement, get everything in writing. If you make a special request, be sure to get that in writing too. It is all too easy after the wedding for the photographer or videographer to come back saying they didn't know or hadn't agreed to something you thought was completely understood.

VIDEO AND PHOTO CHECKLIST

The best way to ensure you get the shots you want is to prepare a checklist for the photographer and videographer, and to assign a friend or relative to point out the relevant people on the day. Use the following ideas as a starting point. Cross off shots you don't want, and add some more of your own. When complete, give a copy to your photographer or videographer.

HOME PORTRAITURE

Bride in her gown

Bride with her father

Bride with her mother

Mother and father of bride

Bride with chief bridesmaid

Bride with her attendants

Bride with both parents

CEREMONY

Groom and best man at altar

Bride and father walking down aisle

Bride and groom at altar

Bride and groom coming up the aisle

Attendants walking down the aisle

Father kissing the bride

Exchange of wedding rings

Signing the register

AFTER THE CEREMONY

Bride and her attendants

Bride with groomsmen

Bride and groom and their families

Groom with his family

Bride and groom with his family

Groom with his father

Groom with both fathers

Mother and father of groom

Groom and his groomsmen

Groom with attendants

Bride with her family

Bride and groom with her family

Entire bridal party and families

Groom with his mother

Bride with both mothers

RECEPTION

Bride and groom dancing

Bride throwing her bouquet

Groom removing bride's garter

The toast

Cutting the cake

Couple leaving

CANDID CAMERA

If you decide against hiring a professional or you prefer to have more natural shots, ask a friend or relative who is a good amateur photographer or videographer to help out on the day. These shots may turn out to be better than professional photos since the person taking them knows you, both your families and friends and may be more in tune with your personalities. A few hints for taking candids follow:

- Use the right equipment — a 35mm camera with automatic focus and built-in flash works best and produces good quality photos.
- Choose the appropriate film — 200ASA film is best for indoors because it can take pictures in very little light. You will also need a high quality videotape for your video camera. Sony VHS cassettes are good quality and widely available.
- Be careful with compositions — take active, rather than passive, shots and ones that express emotion. Try shooting from different angles.
- To get the maximum number of natural shots, try this fun idea. Place one disposable camera (available at most camera shops) at each reception table for guests to take their own shots during the festivities. Attach a note inviting guests to snap away.

AFTER THE WEDDING

After the wedding make an appointment to view the photos and video. Take the checklist and agreement with you in case there are any problems. Traditionally, the bride's family pays for the photographs and video but, if you are ordering albums or copies of the video for both parents, it may be best to split the costs between the two families.

A growing moon and a flowing tide are lucky times to marry in. (Irish saying)

PHOTOGRAPHY ORGANISER

Use this space to compare costs and keep track of your photo information:

Estimate No. 1: Company _____

Photographer _____ Tel. _____

Cancellation policy _____

Cost £ _____ Deposit £ _____

Estimate No. 2: Company _____

Photographer _____ Tel. _____

Cancellation policy _____

Cost £ _____ Deposit £ _____

Estimate No. 3: Company _____

Photographer _____ Tel. _____

Cancellation policy _____

Cost £ _____ Deposit £ _____

Final selection: Company _____

Photographer _____ Tel. _____

Address _____

Cancellation policy _____

Cost £ _____ Deposit £ _____ Balance due £ _____

Selection: Album style _____

Album colour _____

Number of photos _____

NOTES

VIDEO ORGANISER

Use this space to compare costs and keep track of your video information:

Estimate No. 1: Company

Videographer   Tel.

Cancellation policy

Cost £   Deposit £

Estimate No. 2: Company

Videographer   Tel.

Cancellation policy

Cost £   Deposit £

Estimate No. 3: Company

Videographer   Tel.

Cancellation policy

Cost £   Deposit £

Final selection: Company

Videographer   Tel.

Address

Arrival time   Conclusion

Cancellation policy

Cost £   Deposit £   Balance due £

NOTES

18   THE REHEARSAL

As your wedding day draws near you will — hopefully! — start to see all the elements that create a lovely wedding fall into place. The flowers, photographer, reception, pre-marriage course, dress, cake, music and transport have all been ordered, leaving you with one last thing to do — rehearse. If you are having a church wedding, it's important to have a dry run of the ceremony so that everyone knows exactly what is expected of them and when.

ORGANISING THE REHEARSAL

The best time for a rehearsal is the week of the wedding and at the convenience of your celebrant. From start to finish, it should last no more than two hours. Your celebrant should organise the time and date for you and should also be willing to attend the rehearsal. All members of the bridal party, including both sets of parents and the organist or musicians, should be present.

Before the rehearsal, draw up an outline of the wedding day. This may seem excessive, but on the day the participants in your wedding party will really appreciate knowing where they should be, what they will be doing, and at what time. The outline for a one o'clock wedding ceremony might read as follows:

12.00: Ushers arrive at church in full dress and hand out Order of Service/Mass booklets to guests as they arrive. Then, they take guests to their seats on the correct side of the church. Ushers' note: Guests of the bride sit on the left side of the church, guests of the groom on the right.

12.15: Organist/musicians start playing shortly before guests arrive.

12.20: Groom and best man arrive at church in full dress. Best man checks that ushers are ready and wearing their buttonholes.

Best man's note: If there is time before the ceremony, pay the clergy, musicians, bell ringers, etc. Money should be in sealed envelopes.

12.30: Guests arrive.

1.00: Bride, her father, bridesmaids and flower girl arrive and wait outside entrance.

Groom, best man, and groomsmen take their seats in the front right pew (or stand near the altar).

1.05: Mother of groom is ushered to the first pew, behind her son. Groom's father follows.

Bride's mother is ushered to the first pew on the left side of the church.

Organist begins to play the bride's entrance song immediately after the bride's mother is seated.

Bride and her father begin the procession to the altar.

Flower girls and bridesmaids follow in this order: (list names here).

Ceremony begins.

Readings: (put names of readers and their directions here)

Offertory: (names and directions)

Signing of the register: Best man and chief bridesmaid follow bride and groom to the vestry (or altar) to sign the register.

Organist plays a short piece for the signing.

End of ceremony: Celebrant introduces couple to the congregation (optional).

Recessional begins: Organist starts playing the recessional music.

Bride and groom lead the exit.

Best man escorts the chief bridesmaid up the aisle. Groomsmen escort bridesmaids.

Bride's father escorts groom's mother and groom's father escorts bride's mother up the aisle.

2.00: Leave ceremony for reception/photographs.

2.30: Wedding party and parents stand in receiving line and welcome guests. First drinks are served. Photographs are taken.

3.30:   Meal is served.

Best man announces the cutting of the cake. Cake and champagne are
    served to guests.

    Best man reads telegrams and cards, and calls on the father of
    the bride to make the first speech.
    After the father of the bride speaks, the best man calls on the
    groom to speak.
    Groom speaks and thanks the bride's family and toasts the
    bridesmaids.
    Best man stands and thanks the groom for his toast to the
    bridesmaids and makes his own speech.

6.00:   Band announces the first dance.

Hand out the outline at the beginning of the rehearsal. Read out the
important details and then give everyone a few minutes to digest the
rest. The celebrant will describe the ceremony to everyone present
— telling them what to do and when. Ask any questions before the
rehearsal begins, to save time. These are a few of the most likely
questions and their answers:

Is it OK to be late for your wedding?
There is an old Irish custom of the bride being late to her wedding,
but recently this has been sorely abused. It is considered rude to
both guests and clergy for the bride to be more than fifteen minutes
late. If you arrive later than this, do not be surprised if the celebrant
has left the premises.

What does the groom do before the ceremony begins?
Welcome guests, mingle and relax. Once the bridesmaids arrive,
the groom, best man and groomsmen take their seats near the altar.

What are the ushers' responsibilities?
Seat guests as they arrive and hand out Order of Service booklets.
Ushers should ask whether each person is a guest of the bride or
of the groom, and then seat them accordingly. Guests of the bride
sit on the left and guests of the groom on the right. If it is raining,
ushers should have umbrellas and walk guests from their cars to
the church.

When do the mothers take their seats?
An usher should walk the groom's mother to the front right pew once her son takes his seat at the front of the church. The bride's mother is escorted to her seat moments before the ceremony begins.

Which arm does the bride take?
Generally the bride takes her father's right arm so that when they reach the front of the church, he can take his seat on the left without having to cross over her train.

How fast do the attendants walk up the aisle?
Walk slowly, in time with the music, and left foot first. The bride and her father should be half way up the aisle before flower girls and bridesmaids follow. Attendants should keep three to four pews apart when following one another.

THE PROCESSIONAL

This is the order of a traditional Christian processional.

Altar

Clergy

Groom, best man, groomsmen.
Groom, best man and groomsmen stand to the right of the clergy at the altar.

Father of the Bride   Bride
Bride stands to the right of her father and clasps her arm in his.

Child attendants

Flower girls may walk side by side or follow after one another with the youngest child leading. In the case of a ringbearer and flower girl, the boy precedes the girl.

Chief bridesmaid
Bridesmaids

Bridesmaids may follow in order of height, with the tallest first

Once you are at the altar, the celebrant will briefly detail where people will sit or stand throughout the service and describe the ceremony — pointing out to the various members what they do and when. The readers note at what point they stand to give the readings, the best man is reminded at what point he should produce the rings, mothers are told when to bring up the offertory, and so on.

THE RECESSIONAL

In the Christian tradition, the bride and groom lead the walk back up the aisle, followed by bridesmaids, best man and groomsmen. Bridesmaids should know which groomsmen they are paired with. The bride's father should cross the aisle to escort the groom's mother, and the groom's father should do the same for the bride's mother.

Traditional Christian Recessional
Altar

Bride's father	Groom's mother
Bride's mother	Groom's father
Bridesmaid	Groomsman
Bridesmaid	Groomsman
Chief bridesmaid	Best man
Child attendants	
Bride	Groom

At the very end of the rehearsal it is a nice idea to ask the celebrant to say a blessing or prayer. Everyone can do with a little help from up above!

WEDDING EMERGENCIES

You may have organised everything down to the last possible detail, but there will always be something you cannot plan for — missing guests, popped buttons, headaches and forgotten clothes, passports or car keys. The best way to survive a wedding emergency is to be prepared. Some handy tips follow:

- Prepare a small emergency kit which includes clear nail varnish, allergy medicine, aspirin, sewing needles, thread, extra buttons, safety pins, white tape for fallen hems, nail file, extra pair of tights, hair pins, brush or comb, tampons, band aids and tissues.

- Telephone all vendors — photographer, florist, banquet manager, musicians, car hire — the day before the wedding to confirm details.
- Assign a member of your family or close friend to carry a note with the telephone numbers of all your wedding helpers just in case one of them doesn't arrive.
- Be creative. If something doesn't go as you planned, try to find a solution quickly and quietly.
- Relax and smile. At the end of the day what is most important is that the two of you are getting married and having a good time.

PLANNING FOR A RAINY DAY

Regardless of what time of year you marry, the chances are that there will be a few drops of rain. Rain may be an inconvenience, but there are a few ways to work around the weather.

- Ask all the ushers and groomsmen to bring an umbrella to protect guests moving to and from buildings and their cars.
- Put a large umbrella, possibly white, in the bride's car to keep her dry before the ceremony.
- Pack a hairdryer and curling tongs in a bag to be taken to the reception for last minute touch-ups.
- Talk to your photographer about indoor and outdoor photo opportunities.
- Don't unroll the aisle runner until guests have taken their seats.
- If your reception is at home, hire a marquee or have a back-up indoor plan.

An old Irish custom is that the groom presented the bride with some newly churned country butter beside a mill, a tree or a stream — all symbols of endurance. Thereupon he recited this prayer: O Woman loved by me, mayest thou give me thy heart, thy soul, thy body.

19   THE HONEYMOON

The Irish for honeymoon *'Mí na meala'*, literally month of honey, harks back to the days when couples drank a honey wine for a full cycle of the moon after they wed — hence the word honeymoon. Though we don't do this today, a holiday at home or abroad is still a great way to top off a wedding celebration.

MAKING PLANS

Your biggest decision is where to go. This depends largely on your budget and the amount of time you can take off work. When you work for yourself getting time off is easy, but otherwise you should try to book holiday time soon after the engagement. If one or both of you must go back to work immediately, try to take at least a day or two off for yourselves, or make plans for the first long weekend.

Deciding where to go is usually the fun part. If you have nowhere specific in mind, contact travel agents for brochures. Alternatively, buy some good travel magazines and see if anywhere catches your imagination. Once you have narrowed down the possibilities start researching them at the library or bookshop. If you are interested in visiting a foreign country, telephone their tourist office, consulate or embassy and ask them to send you information.

Even if your budget is small, there are still many opportunities for a memorable honeymoon. If you have your hearts set on a rather expensive trip, discreetly let family and friends know that you would prefer a gift of money in lieu of another present. Of course, it is ultimately their decision, but many will be delighted to contribute to your holiday. Travelling outside Ireland can be less expensive if you go during off-peak times or don't travel direct. A travel agent is the best source of such information. Also, ask close friends and relatives if they have a holiday home you could borrow or rent at a reduced rate. Keep in mind that campgrounds, self-catering apartments and B&Bs are much less expensive than hotels. Or think about travelling via London — many flights out of London are considerably cheaper than from Ireland, and there is a greater choice of destination.

Another possibility is right here at home. Ireland has beautiful cities and villages to explore. You'll save on travel costs as well as fees for passports, visas, vaccinations and foreign exchange. Contact Bord Fáilte for some suggestions.

Once you have selected a destination you will need to book accommodation, transport and, possibly, a car for touring around. A good travel agent should be able to arrange all these details. Since their fee is paid by the airlines and hotels you should not have to pay for their assistance.

One easy way to avoid having to book different details is to take a package holiday. Typically, you can expect return tickets, accommodation and meals all for one price. This is particularly good for those on a tight budget as all the costs are set before you go. There may be a few extra fees such as tax, tips, sightseeing and airport transfers, but these are usually nominal.

HOW TO GET THERE

Obviously travelling by air is the quickest and easiest method to most destinations. For travel to the UK, consider going by ferry as this is usually less expensive and reasonably convenient. When going by air, there are a few things you should do to ensure your flight is as pleasant as possible.

First, before you make a reservation be sure to ask about discount fares. Most airlines and travel agents hold back a number of lower priced seats, so make sure you are getting the best deal possible. Always ask if the price quoted is the lowest fare available. Generally, you need to book seven, fourteen or twenty-one days in advance and you have to stay at least one week (requiring one Saturday night stay-over) to qualify for a less expensive ticket.

Find out whether your flight is direct or non-stop. Non-stop flights have no stop-overs between destinations, while direct flights may touchdown en route though you don't have to change planes.

Request boarding passes and seat assignments when the tickets are issued. This will save you the trouble of trying to get a seat together or a window or aisle seat on the day of your flight. Although getting boarding passes in advance is not possible in Ireland, be sure to ask when travelling in other countries.

If you are a gold or platinum card holder of a frequent flyer programme, be sure to ask about automatic upgrades. Because you are a valued customer, you are more likely to be moved into a higher class of service.

Another detail the airlines and travel agents don't readily share is the fact that you can order special meals. Vegetarian, fat-free, low cholesterol, seafood and others are often available. Requests should be made at the time of booking or not less than forty-eight hours before departure.

When booking the flight and checking in, mention that this is your honeymoon flight. Some airlines will surprise you by upgrading your seats on the day or bringing you a bottle of champagne as their way of saying congratulations.

On the day you fly, telephone the airline two to four hours before the flight leaves to ensure that it is leaving on time. Arrive at the airport at least one-and-a-half hours before the flight leaves. This should ensure that you don't get bumped from the flight because of overbooking and that your luggage gets checked in and loaded on the right plane.

TOURING AROUND

Once you arrive at your destination and settle in, you may want to see the sights. You could walk but you will see more if you rent a car.

Before you go out and accept the first deal you are offered, shop around. Compare daily and weekly rates and ask about any special rates. Enquire about the hidden costs — insurance, petrol, drop-off charge and late return. It might be convenient for you to hire at one place and drop off at another, such as the airport. Some companies have no extra charge for this. Do not pay for insurance or collision coverage if you already have a policy which protects you. Some credit card companies automatically cover you if you refuse additional insurance when renting.

When you book the car, be sure to ask for a confirmation number as this will help you if there are any problems when you arrive. When you pick the car up, ask the agent for a map of the area and go over a few rules of the road like speed limits and parking. Before you drive off, take a look at the car. Check for dents, scratches, interior damage and whether the petrol tank is full or empty. If there is any doubt in your mind, report it: better safe than sorry.

DOCUMENTS

If you plan to travel outside Ireland for your honeymoon, you may need passports and visas. To apply for passports, go to a local garda station and ask for an application form (one per person is required). Fill in the application, attach two passport-size photographs (colour or black and white) to each application and ask a garda to sign both the photos and the applications. Next, send the completed forms, photos and your out-of-date passport, if you have one, to the Passport Office, Setanta Centre, Molesworth Street, Dublin 2, with a cheque for £45. Within about four to five weeks your passport, valid for ten years, will be sent out to you.

If you decide to change your surname, you have two options. You can apply for a new passport, following the above procedure but including your marriage certificate. Or, you can leave your current passport as it is, have any tickets for the honeymoon issued in your maiden name, and make the changes when you return.

Some countries require a visa in addition to your passport. Check with your travel agent or telephone the embassy or consulate of the country you plan to visit to find out what documentation is needed.

MONEY

Whether you take a little or a lot, you can never be too careful with your honeymoon money. The safest way to carry money is in the form of traveller's cheques which are accepted like cash in most countries but safer because they can be replaced if lost or stolen. Shop around for the best deal, which is often your own bank. Find out how quickly your money will be refunded if lost or stolen, or what happens if your passport or identification is lost as well. Ask where the company's nearest office is in the country you are visiting. Their service will be of little use if their office is too far away.

When you buy the cheques, you will be given a receipt for each one with a serial number on it. Keep these separate from the cheques and in a safe place. If you need to replace them for whatever reason you will have to provide the receipts as proof of purchase and ownership.

Credit cards are another way to travel without carrying large sums of money. Write down the name, account number and emergency telephone number of each card before travelling and put it in a safe place. And, before you go, pay any outstanding balances on your cards so you have the freedom to use them as you wish.

INSURANCE

Accidents and problems are the last thing you want to think about — buy some insurance and ensure a carefree trip. Your travel agent or tour operator will recommend a package covering health, loss of luggage and travel delay. A comprehensive package usually costs between £20 and £40.

LUGGAGE

Your honeymoon is a good excuse to buy a new set of luggage. If you decide to do so, go for quality: good luggage is an investment and you don't want the hassle of broken zips and faulty handles. If you are not sure what pieces to start with, a good choice is one medium sized hard case, which should hold two weeks worth of clothes for one person, and a medium sized soft case which can be hand carried or checked in. Also, consider a garment bag. If buying a new one, look for extra features such as hangers which lock in place so clothes won't slide inside the bag and pockets for carrying bulky items like shoes and a hairdryer.

Before you pack, find out if there are any baggage restrictions. It is terribly irritating, not to mention expensive, to learn you are over the limit when you're checking-in. Your travel agent should be able to give you this information.

Take a few minutes at check-in to go over your baggage. Check for damage, slipping locks and loose straps. If you have over-packed and the zip is pulling at the sides, ask the check-in assistant for packing tape. Cut pieces of tape the length of the zip and cover it well — this won't guarantee the loss of any items but it will help. Lastly, label your bags and if possible, use your business address as a safety precaution.

If you are driving or hiking on your honeymoon, you might want to consider purchasing waterproof luggage just in case of bad weather. Alternatively, bring large plastic refuse sacks and cover your bags when necessary.

WHAT TO PACK

The age-old problem — one of you over-packs and the other has to help carry. A good solution is to agree early on that you carry what you pack. This not only cuts down on the arguments but it is also gentler on your back! Here are a few tips for scaling down the bulk:

- Find out the temperature and climate of your destination for both day and night and pack accordingly. (A travel agent should be able to tell you.)
- Select two basic colours for your clothes and take separates that mix and match. If an item doesn't go with at least two others, leave it behind.
- Pack accessories. Use them to change the mood or style of your outfits and add a bit of colour.
- Don't pack clothes which wrinkle easily. This means leaving linens, silks, and some 100% cottons behind: instead, opt for wools, cotton blends, and synthetic materials.
- To avoid wrinkles, wrap your clothes in tissue paper. Your local dry cleaner might give it to you free if asked nicely.
- Let some clothes do double duty. Stuff shoes inside socks or use socks to help keep the shape of shoes, suits or dresses.
- Use ziplock bags to keep cologne, shampoo, suntan oil, make-up, etc. from spoiling your clothes while in transit.
- Don't forget essential items (such as umbrella, sunscreen, sunglasses) and recreational items (Walkman, books, cards, tennis racket, etc.)
- A secret borrowed from air hostesses is to pack clothes as flat as possible — the roll theory is out.
- Bring a lightweight duffle bag for those purchases you make while you're away.
- In your hand luggage pack any medication, a few personal items and a change of clothes in case your luggage goes astray.

HONEYMOON COUNTDOWN

To make the most of your honeymoon, try to organise details before you leave. The following countdown will help you remember what needs to be done.

THREE MONTHS BEFORE

- Begin researching honeymoon destinations. Check with friends or travel agents for package tours and read travel magazines for ideas.
- Determine your holiday budget.
- Decide how many days you can take off and put in a request for holidays at work.
- Agree on a destination.
- Contact a travel agent to book flights, accommodation, car rental and any other details you require, or start organising the details yourselves. Have confirmations sent to you in writing.
- Update or apply for passports and visas, if necessary.
- Visit your doctor for a check-up and find out what vaccinations, if any, you need.

TWO MONTHS BEFORE

- If you have not received your travel confirmations, telephone.
- Decide whether or not you need to buy new luggage and make any necessary purchases.
- Go through your wardrobe and decide which clothes to take with you. If you need any new clothes, now is the time to start shopping.

ONE MONTH BEFORE

- Check to see that your camera is in good working condition. Buy film and extra batteries.
- Have your tickets sent to your home. Keep them together with your passports and visas.
- If you are driving your own car on your honeymoon, have it serviced or repaired.
- Make a list of the items you want to take with you. Don't forget to pack the essentials — sunscreen, sunglasses, band-aids, aspirin, etc.
- If you take any medication, check that you have enough to last

for the trip.
- Pay bills that will fall due while you're away.
- Check to see that your credit cards are valid for the duration of your holiday and check your current credit limit. If necessary, pay off any outstanding balance.
- Ask a neighbour to keep an eye on your house, car and pets while you are away.

ONE WEEK BEFORE
- Buy traveller's cheques and local currency. Keep the receipts in a separate but safe place.
- For easy access, put all important documents — passports, visas, tickets, traveller's cheques — in one place.
- Pack and label your luggage.
- Reconfirm travel plans.
- Pick up maps of the area you are visiting and take time to go over them together.

DAY OF TRAVEL
- If driving your own car, fill the petrol tank.
- Phone airline, ferry, train stations etc to confirm departure time.
- Check that you have tickets, money, passports, visas and any medication with you.
- Get to the airport, train station etc, with enough time to check in.
- Relax. Bon voyage!

- Before you return, phone a few days in advance to confirm return flights or other travel arrangements.

Sweetly speaking, witty, clear,
Tribe most lovely to my mind,
Blame of such I hate to hear.
Speak not ill of womankind.

Bloody treason, murderous act,
Not by women were designed,
Bells o'erthrown nor churches sacked
Speak not ill of womankind.

These lines were written in honour of Eleanor Butler in 1565 when the Earl of Desmond fell in love with her. Their marriage got off to a head start, making her Countess of Desmond, with a large dowry from her father and gifts from her husband of the town and castle of Bridgesford, Co Tipperary.
(from Eleanor, Countess of Desmond by Anne Chambers)

HONEYMOON ORGANISER

Use this honeymoon planner to organise the details of your trip:

Dates of honeymoon

Budget £

Possible destinations

Travel agent

Contact   Tel.

Destination

Address & tel. of accommodation

Notes

Car rental company   Tel.

Type   Cost £

Notes

Passports

Visas

Vaccinations

NOTES

20   POST-WEDDING DETAILS

It was a great wedding! All your hard work and effort paid off. Everyone said it was the most enjoyable wedding day they had ever celebrated. Now you can sit back and relax. Right? Not yet. There are still a few details which need your attention.

THANK-YOU NOTES

Try to write and send thank-you notes to people who have sent you gifts within a week of receiving them. If you are lucky enough to receive lots of gifts, it helps to stay on top of the task if you write these as you go along. If you receive gifts on your wedding day, or shortly before, you can write when you return from honeymoon.

Some couples like the idea of sending pre-printed thank-you cards. This is a fast way of acknowledging a gift, but it is not an acceptable way of showing your appreciation. All gifts should be acknowledged with a personal, handwritten note. Individual attention is difficult when you have already written twenty other thank-you notes, but a nice note will make the giver feel that you really appreciate his or her present. Mention the gift and try to make reference to its place in your new home. For example:

Dear Maureen,
Brian and I would like to thank you for the fabulous wok you gave us on our wedding day. You're great to remember how much we like Chinese food. Brian can't wait to give it a go with his favourite stir-fry recipe.
Please let us know the next time you are in Galway. We'd love to have you over for dinner.
Thanks again!
Siobhán

PRESERVING YOUR GOWN

To preserve your wedding dress have it professionally cleaned as soon as possible. If you are going away on honeymoon, ask your mother or bridesmaid to take it to the cleaners the week after the wedding. If there are any stains, be sure to let the cleaners know so they can pre-treat them.

When you get the dress back, stuff the bodice and arms with white acid-free tissue paper. If you are storing it on a hanger, sew straps to the inside of the waistline to provide extra support so it won't stretch. Wrap the dress in a white sheet or muslin and hang in a cool, dry place. Alternatively, fold it up in a large box stuffed with white acid-free paper. Put the box in a cotton bag and keep in a cool, dry place. Check the condition of the gown from time to time.

DAILY MEMORIES

You may like to keep a memento of your wedding with you through-out the year. Some ways of doing so include lining your dresser drawers with some of the wrapping paper from your wedding gifts, turning the lucky penny you wore in your wedding shoe into a key chain or charm, having your invitation transferred on to a collector's plate or cross stitch pillow, wearing a locket with a wedding picture in it, or displaying your cake-top ornament in a glass box.

ORDER YOUR PHOTOGRAPHS

Your photographer should have samples or contact sheets of the best of your wedding day photos for you to see within two weeks of the wedding. Look through them together. If money is tight, don't order an album for each set of parents. Instead, pick two or three of the best photographs and frame them yourselves. Alternatively, invite your parents to go with you and let them order the ones they want.

POST-WEDDING BLUES

After all the excitement and stress leading up to the wedding, the weeks and months afterwards may seem like a disappointment. If you are feeling anxious or out of sorts, don't fret. These feelings, known as post-wedding blues, are fairly common and very curable!

Recognise the symptoms for what they are — physical, emotional and mental exhaustion. The best medicine is relaxation. Take time out for yourself — read a good book, take an evening walk, get to bed early. Talk to your partner and let him or her know how you feel. Keeping feelings hidden will only cause undue stress. Before you know it, you will be back to your old self in no time.

NOTIFICATION OF CHANGE OF ADDRESS

If you move to a new address, don't forget to let friends, relatives, and others know. Card shops have lovely pre-printed change-of-address cards: packets of ten usually cost about £5.

IMPORTANT RECORDS

If you have changed your name, notify your banks, the ESB, credit card companies, Telecom and any organisations who are in regular contact with you, or can influence your credit rating. You should also consider changing your passport to simplify things when you travel.

INSURANCE AND WILLS

None of us likes to think about something going wrong but it is always better to be prepared than caught off guard. Look into car, household, health and life insurance and upgrade any policies you currently hold to meet your new needs. Like insurance, a will is necessary to ensure the security of your loved ones. To make a will, contact your solicitor.

ANNIVERSARIES

In the years to come the two of you will look back on your wedding day with special fondness. To give the years together extra meaning and fun, try to keep these anniversary traditions.

One: Paper	*Eleven:* Steel	
Two: Cotton	*Twelve:* Linen	*Twenty-five:* Silver
Three: Leather	*Thirteen:* Lace	*Thirty:* Pearl
Four: Silk	*Fourteen:* Ivory	*Thirty-five:* Coral
Five: Wood	*Fifteen:* Crystal	*Forty:* Ruby
Six: Iron	*Sixteen:* Sterling	*Forty-five:* Sapphire
Seven: Wool	*Seventeen:* Furniture	*Fifty:* Gold
Eight: Bronze	*Eighteen:* Porcelain	*Fifty-five:* Emerald
Nine: Pottery	*Nineteen:* Bronze	Sixty: Diamond
Ten: Tin	*Twenty:* China	

INDEX